Data Centric Audit
Complete Self-Assessment Guide

C000171061

The guidance in this Self-Assessment is based
practices and standards in business process a............., ...g
quality management. The guidance is also based on the professional
judgment of the individual collaborators listed in the Acknowledgments.

Notice of rights

Trademarks

Table of Contents

About The Art of Service

The Art of Service, Business Process Architects since 2000, is dedicated to helping stakeholders achieve excellence.

Defining, designing, creating, and implementing a process to solve a stakeholders challenge or meet an objective is the most valuable role… In EVERY group, company, organization and department.

Unless you're talking a one-time, single-use project, there should be a process. Whether that process is managed and implemented by humans, AI, or a combination of the two, it needs to be designed by someone with a complex enough perspective to ask the right questions.

Someone capable of asking the right questions and step back and say, 'What are we really trying to accomplish here? And is there a different way to look at it?'

With The Art of Service's Standard Requirements Self-Assessments, we empower people who can do just that — whether their title is marketer, entrepreneur, manager, salesperson, consultant, Business Process Manager, executive assistant, IT Manager, CIO etc... —they are the people who rule the future. They are people who watch the process as it happens, and ask the right questions to make the process work better.

Contact us when you need any support with this Self-Assessment and any help with templates, blue-prints and examples of standard documents you might need:

http://theartofservice.com
service@theartofservice.com

Included Resources - how to access

Included with your purchase of the book is the Data Centric

Audit Self-Assessment Spreadsheet Dashboard which contains all questions and Self-Assessment areas and auto-generates insights, graphs, and project RACI planning - all with examples to get you started right away.

How? Simply send an email to
access@theartofservice.com
with this books' title in the subject to get the Data Centric Audit Self Assessment Tool right away.

You will receive the following contents with New and Updated specific criteria:

- The latest quick edition of the book in PDF

- The latest complete edition of the book in PDF, which criteria correspond to the criteria in...

- The Self-Assessment Excel Dashboard, and...

- Example pre-filled Self-Assessment Excel Dashboard to get familiar with results generation

- In-depth specific Checklists covering the topic

- Project management checklists and templates to assist with implementation

INCLUDES LIFETIME SELF ASSESSMENT UPDATES

Every self assessment comes with Lifetime Updates and Lifetime Free Updated Books. Lifetime Updates is an industry-first feature which allows you to receive verified self assessment updates, ensuring you always have the most accurate information at your fingertips.

Get it now- you will be glad you did - do it now, before you forget.

Send an email to **access@theartofservice.com** with this books' title in the subject to get the Data Centric Audit Self Assessment Tool right away.

Purpose of this Self-Assessment

This Self-Assessment has been developed to improve understanding of the requirements and elements of Data Centric Audit, based on best practices and standards in business process architecture, design and quality management.

It is designed to allow for a rapid Self-Assessment to determine how closely existing management practices and procedures correspond to the elements of the Self-Assessment.

The criteria of requirements and elements of Data Centric Audit have been rephrased in the format of a Self-Assessment questionnaire, with a seven-criterion scoring system, as explained in this document.

In this format, even with limited background knowledge of Data Centric Audit, a manager can quickly review existing operations to determine how they measure up to the standards. This in turn can serve as the starting point of a 'gap analysis' to identify management tools or system elements that might usefully be implemented in the organization to help improve overall performance.

How to use the Self-Assessment

On the following pages are a series of questions to identify to what extent your Data Centric Audit initiative is complete in comparison to the requirements set in standards.

To facilitate answering the questions, there is a space in front of each question to enter a score on a scale of '1' to '5'.

1 Strongly Disagree

2 Disagree

3 Neutral

4 Agree

5 Strongly Agree

Read the question and rate it with the following in front of mind:

'In my belief, the answer to this question is clearly defined'.

There are two ways in which you can choose to interpret this statement;

1. how aware are you that the answer to the question is clearly defined
2. for more in-depth analysis you can choose to gather evidence and confirm the answer to the question. This obviously will take more time, most Self-Assessment users opt for the first way to interpret the question and dig deeper later on based on the outcome of the overall Self-Assessment.

A score of '1' would mean that the answer is not clear at all, where a '5' would mean the answer is crystal clear and defined. Leave emtpy when the question is not applicable or you don't want to answer it, you can skip it without affecting your score. Write your score in the space provided.

After you have responded to all the appropriate statements in each section, compute your average score for that section, using the formula provided, and round to the nearest tenth. Then transfer to the corresponding spoke in the Data Centric Audit Scorecard on the second next page of the Self-Assessment.

Your completed Data Centric Audit Scorecard will give you a clear presentation of which Data Centric Audit areas need attention.

Data Centric Audit
Scorecard Example

Example of how the finalized Scorecard can look like:

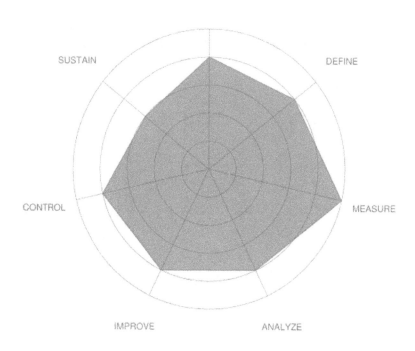

Data Centric Audit Scorecard

Your Scores:

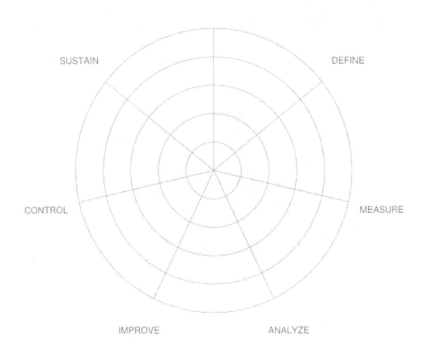

**BEGINNING OF THE
SELF-ASSESSMENT:**

CRITERION #1: RECOGNIZE

INTENT: Be aware of the need for change. Recognize that there is an unfavorable variation, problem or symptom.

In my belief, the answer to this question is clearly defined:

5 Strongly Agree

4 Agree

3 Neutral

2 Disagree

1 Strongly Disagree

1. What does data centric audit success mean to the stakeholders?
<--- Score

2. To what extent does each concerned units management team recognize data centric audit as an effective investment?
<--- Score

3. What are the clients issues and concerns?
<--- Score

4. Is the need for organizational change recognized?
<--- Score

5. Is it needed?
<--- Score

6. What is the data centric audit problem definition? What do you need to resolve?
<--- Score

7. Who should resolve the data centric audit issues?
<--- Score

8. What are the expected benefits of data centric audit to the stakeholder?
<--- Score

9. What is the recognized need?
<--- Score

10. Are losses recognized in a timely manner?
<--- Score

11. Are controls defined to recognize and contain problems?
<--- Score

12. How are training requirements identified?
<--- Score

13. How does it fit into your organizational needs and tasks?

<--- Score

14. Where do you need to exercise leadership?
<--- Score

15. What vendors make products that address the data centric audit needs?
<--- Score

16. Who are your key stakeholders who need to sign off?
<--- Score

17. Looking at each person individually – does every one have the qualities which are needed to work in this group?
<--- Score

18. What data centric audit problem should be solved?
<--- Score

19. How many trainings, in total, are needed?
<--- Score

20. Are there recognized data centric audit problems?
<--- Score

21. Would you recognize a threat from the inside?
<--- Score

22. What activities does the governance board need to consider?
<--- Score

23. How much are sponsors, customers, partners,

stakeholders involved in data centric audit? In other words, what are the risks, if data centric audit does not deliver successfully?
<--- Score

24. Are you dealing with any of the same issues today as yesterday? What can you do about this?
<--- Score

25. Who else hopes to benefit from it?
<--- Score

26. What is the smallest subset of the problem you can usefully solve?
<--- Score

27. Who needs what information?
<--- Score

28. What is the problem and/or vulnerability?
<--- Score

29. Think about the people you identified for your data centric audit project and the project responsibilities you would assign to them, what kind of training do you think they would need to perform these responsibilities effectively?
<--- Score

30. Are there regulatory / compliance issues?
<--- Score

31. Why the need?
<--- Score

32. What situation(s) led to this data centric audit Self

Assessment?
<--- Score

33. Are your goals realistic? Do you need to redefine your problem? Perhaps the problem has changed or maybe you have reached your goal and need to set a new one?
<--- Score

34. What would happen if data centric audit weren't done?
<--- Score

35. What are the minority interests and what amount of minority interests can be recognized?
<--- Score

36. Do you need different information or graphics?
<--- Score

37. To what extent would your organization benefit from being recognized as a award recipient?
<--- Score

38. How do you recognize an objection?
<--- Score

39. Why is this needed?
<--- Score

40. As a sponsor, customer or management, how important is it to meet goals, objectives?
<--- Score

41. Have you identified your data centric audit key performance indicators?

<--- Score

42. Are there any specific expectations or concerns about the data centric audit team, data centric audit itself?
<--- Score

43. What do employees need in the short term?
<--- Score

44. What is the extent or complexity of the data centric audit problem?
<--- Score

45. How are you going to measure success?
<--- Score

46. What do you need to start doing?
<--- Score

47. Does the problem have ethical dimensions?
<--- Score

48. Consider your own data centric audit project, what types of organizational problems do you think might be causing or affecting your problem, based on the work done so far?
<--- Score

49. What needs to stay?
<--- Score

50. Can management personnel recognize the monetary benefit of data centric audit?
<--- Score

51. Do you have/need 24-hour access to key personnel?
<--- Score

52. What are the data centric audit resources needed?
<--- Score

53. How do you assess your data centric audit workforce capability and capacity needs, including skills, competencies, and staffing levels?
<--- Score

54. What are the timeframes required to resolve each of the issues/problems?
<--- Score

55. What are your needs in relation to data centric audit skills, labor, equipment, and markets?
<--- Score

56. How are the data centric audit's objectives aligned to the group's overall stakeholder strategy?
<--- Score

57. How do you take a forward-looking perspective in identifying data centric audit research related to market response and models?
<--- Score

58. Does data centric audit create potential expectations in other areas that need to be recognized and considered?
<--- Score

59. Will it solve real problems?
<--- Score

60. Are employees recognized or rewarded for performance that demonstrates the highest levels of integrity?
<--- Score

61. Is it clear when you think of the day ahead of you what activities and tasks you need to complete?
<--- Score

62. Will new equipment/products be required to facilitate data centric audit delivery, for example is new software needed?
<--- Score

63. Are there any revenue recognition issues?
<--- Score

64. Do you need to avoid or amend any data centric audit activities?
<--- Score

65. How can auditing be a preventative security measure?
<--- Score

66. What data centric audit capabilities do you need?
<--- Score

67. Will data centric audit deliverables need to be tested and, if so, by whom?
<--- Score

68. What should be considered when identifying available resources, constraints, and deadlines?

<--- Score

69. Where is training needed?
<--- Score

70. How do you recognize an data centric audit objection?
<--- Score

71. Are problem definition and motivation clearly presented?
<--- Score

72. What problems are you facing and how do you consider data centric audit will circumvent those obstacles?
<--- Score

73. Who defines the rules in relation to any given issue?
<--- Score

74. Did you miss any major data centric audit issues?
<--- Score

75. What data centric audit coordination do you need?
<--- Score

76. Is the quality assurance team identified?
<--- Score

77. Do you recognize data centric audit achievements?
<--- Score

78. Are employees recognized for desired behaviors?

<--- Score

79. Which issues are too important to ignore?
<--- Score

80. What data centric audit events should you attend?
<--- Score

81. Will a response program recognize when a crisis occurs and provide some level of response?
<--- Score

82. Do you know what you need to know about data centric audit?
<--- Score

83. Who needs to know?
<--- Score

84. How do you identify subcontractor relationships?
<--- Score

85. Who needs to know about data centric audit?
<--- Score

86. Whom do you really need or want to serve?
<--- Score

87. Which information does the data centric audit business case need to include?
<--- Score

88. What creative shifts do you need to take?
<--- Score

89. What tools and technologies are needed for a

custom data centric audit project?
<--- Score

90. What needs to be done?
<--- Score

91. What are the stakeholder objectives to be achieved with data centric audit?
<--- Score

92. What resources or support might you need?
<--- Score

93. For your data centric audit project, identify and describe the business environment, is there more than one layer to the business environment?
<--- Score

94. Are there data centric audit problems defined?
<--- Score

95. What else needs to be measured?
<--- Score

96. What prevents you from making the changes you know will make you a more effective data centric audit leader?
<--- Score

Add up total points for this section:
_____ = Total points for this section

Divided by: _____ (number of statements answered) = _____
Average score for this section

Transfer your score to the data centric
audit Index at the beginning of the
Self-Assessment.

CRITERION #2: DEFINE:

INTENT: Formulate the stakeholder problem. Define the problem, needs and objectives.

In my belief, the answer to this question is clearly defined:

5 Strongly Agree

4 Agree

3 Neutral

2 Disagree

1 Strongly Disagree

1. How often are the team meetings?
<--- Score

2. How was the 'as is' process map developed, reviewed, verified and validated?
<--- Score

3. How do you manage scope?
<--- Score

4. Has a data centric audit requirement not been met?
<--- Score

5. What is in scope?
<--- Score

6. What is the worst case scenario?
<--- Score

7. What is the scope of the data centric audit work?
<--- Score

8. How does the data centric audit manager ensure against scope creep?
<--- Score

9. What data centric audit services do you require?
<--- Score

10. What would be the goal or target for a data centric audit's improvement team?
<--- Score

11. What is the definition of data centric audit excellence?
<--- Score

12. Is the data centric audit scope manageable?
<--- Score

13. What is the scope?
<--- Score

14. What specifically is the problem? Where does it occur? When does it occur? What is its extent?

<--- Score

15. Is there a data centric audit management charter, including stakeholder case, problem and goal statements, scope, milestones, roles and responsibilities, communication plan?
<--- Score

16. Has a project plan, Gantt chart, or similar been developed/completed?
<--- Score

17. Are roles and responsibilities formally defined?
<--- Score

18. What are the core elements of the data centric audit business case?
<--- Score

19. What sources do you use to gather information for a data centric audit study?
<--- Score

20. What are the record-keeping requirements of data centric audit activities?
<--- Score

21. Have the customer needs been translated into specific, measurable requirements? How?
<--- Score

22. How do you gather data centric audit requirements?
<--- Score

23. What is out of scope?

<--- Score

24. Is special data centric audit user knowledge required?
<--- Score

25. When are meeting minutes sent out? Who is on the distribution list?
<--- Score

26. When is/was the data centric audit start date?
<--- Score

27. What are the data centric audit tasks and definitions?
<--- Score

28. Is there a clear data centric audit case definition?
<--- Score

29. What is the definition of success?
<--- Score

30. Who approved the data centric audit scope?
<--- Score

31. How did the data centric audit manager receive input to the development of a data centric audit improvement plan and the estimated completion dates/times of each activity?
<--- Score

32. What baselines are required to be defined and managed?
<--- Score

33. Why are you doing data centric audit and what is the scope?
<--- Score

34. Where can you gather more information?
<--- Score

35. How do you think the partners involved in data centric audit would have defined success?
<--- Score

36. What are the tasks and definitions?
<--- Score

37. What key stakeholder process output measure(s) does data centric audit leverage and how?
<--- Score

38. Does the scope remain the same?
<--- Score

39. What data centric audit requirements should be gathered?
<--- Score

40. Who defines (or who defined) the rules and roles?
<--- Score

41. How would you define data centric audit leadership?
<--- Score

42. What are the requirements for audit information?
<--- Score

43. What scope to assess?
<--- Score

44. What is the scope of data centric audit?
<--- Score

45. What are the rough order estimates on cost savings/opportunities that data centric audit brings?
<--- Score

46. Are there any constraints known that bear on the ability to perform data centric audit work? How is the team addressing them?
<--- Score

47. What customer feedback methods were used to solicit their input?
<--- Score

48. In what way can you redefine the criteria of choice clients have in your category in your favor?
<--- Score

49. What intelligence can you gather?
<--- Score

50. What information do you gather?
<--- Score

51. Is data centric audit required?
<--- Score

52. The political context: who holds power?
<--- Score

53. Is there any additional data centric audit definition of success?
<--- Score

54. How have you defined all data centric audit requirements first?
<--- Score

55. Are resources adequate for the scope?
<--- Score

56. Has everyone on the team, including the team leaders, been properly trained?
<--- Score

57. Is the data centric audit scope complete and appropriately sized?
<--- Score

58. Is data collected and displayed to better understand customer(s) critical needs and requirements.
<--- Score

59. How do you keep key subject matter experts in the loop?
<--- Score

60. Are the data centric audit requirements testable?
<--- Score

61. How do you gather requirements?
<--- Score

62. How will variation in the actual durations of each activity be dealt with to ensure that the expected data

centric audit results are met?
<--- Score

63. Will a data centric audit production readiness review be required?
<--- Score

64. What information should you gather?
<--- Score

65. Is scope creep really all bad news?
<--- Score

66. Is the scope of data centric audit defined?
<--- Score

67. When is the estimated completion date?
<--- Score

68. How would you define the culture at your organization, how susceptible is it to data centric audit changes?
<--- Score

69. Are task requirements clearly defined?
<--- Score

70. Has anyone else (internal or external to the group) attempted to solve this problem or a similar one before? If so, what knowledge can be leveraged from these previous efforts?
<--- Score

71. What is the scope of the data centric audit effort?
<--- Score

72. Are audit criteria, scope, frequency and methods defined?
<--- Score

73. Are approval levels defined for contracts and supplements to contracts?
<--- Score

74. Scope of sensitive information?
<--- Score

75. Do you have organizational privacy requirements?
<--- Score

76. Has/have the customer(s) been identified?
<--- Score

77. Who is gathering information?
<--- Score

78. What system do you use for gathering data centric audit information?
<--- Score

79. Is the current 'as is' process being followed? If not, what are the discrepancies?
<--- Score

80. What gets examined?
<--- Score

81. How are consistent data centric audit definitions important?
<--- Score

82. Are accountability and ownership for data centric

audit clearly defined?
<--- Score

83. Is the team adequately staffed with the desired cross-functionality? If not, what additional resources are available to the team?
<--- Score

84. What happens if data centric audit's scope changes?
<--- Score

85. Is data centric audit linked to key stakeholder goals and objectives?
<--- Score

86. What are (control) requirements for data centric audit Information?
<--- Score

87. Has the data centric audit work been fairly and/ or equitably divided and delegated among team members who are qualified and capable to perform the work? Has everyone contributed?
<--- Score

88. Is data centric audit currently on schedule according to the plan?
<--- Score

89. Are all requirements met?
<--- Score

90. What are the data centric audit use cases?
<--- Score

91. How do you manage unclear data centric audit requirements?
<--- Score

92. What are the boundaries of the scope? What is in bounds and what is not? What is the start point? What is the stop point?
<--- Score

93. Who are the data centric audit improvement team members, including Management Leads and Coaches?
<--- Score

94. Does the team have regular meetings?
<--- Score

95. What scope do you want your strategy to cover?
<--- Score

96. How will the data centric audit team and the group measure complete success of data centric audit?
<--- Score

97. Is there a critical path to deliver data centric audit results?
<--- Score

98. Are different versions of process maps needed to account for the different types of inputs?
<--- Score

99. What is a worst-case scenario for losses?
<--- Score

100. Is the improvement team aware of the different versions of a process: what they think it is vs. what it actually is vs. what it should be vs. what it could be?
<--- Score

101. What are the compelling stakeholder reasons for embarking on data centric audit?
<--- Score

102. If substitutes have been appointed, have they been briefed on the data centric audit goals and received regular communications as to the progress to date?
<--- Score

103. Has the direction changed at all during the course of data centric audit? If so, when did it change and why?
<--- Score

104. Is there regularly 100% attendance at the team meetings? If not, have appointed substitutes attended to preserve cross-functionality and full representation?
<--- Score

105. How do you catch data centric audit definition inconsistencies?
<--- Score

106. What is out-of-scope initially?
<--- Score

107. How do you build the right business case?
<--- Score

108. Is there a completed SIPOC representation, describing the Suppliers, Inputs, Process, Outputs, and Customers?
<--- Score

109. Has your scope been defined?
<--- Score

110. What is the context?
<--- Score

111. Are required metrics defined, what are they?
<--- Score

112. Do you have a data centric audit success story or case study ready to tell and share?
<--- Score

113. What are the Roles and Responsibilities for each team member and its leadership? Where is this documented?
<--- Score

114. Have all basic functions of data centric audit been defined?
<--- Score

115. What was the context?
<--- Score

116. Has a team charter been developed and communicated?
<--- Score

117. Are there different segments of customers?
<--- Score

118. How do you gather the stories?
<--- Score

119. How do you manage changes in data centric audit requirements?
<--- Score

120. How is the team tracking and documenting its work?
<--- Score

121. How can the value of data centric audit be defined?
<--- Score

122. What constraints exist that might impact the team?
<--- Score

123. Do you all define data centric audit in the same way?
<--- Score

124. Do the problem and goal statements meet the SMART criteria (specific, measurable, attainable, relevant, and time-bound)?
<--- Score

125. Is it clearly defined in and to your organization what you do?
<--- Score

126. Has a high-level 'as is' process map been completed, verified and validated?
<--- Score

127. Is there a completed, verified, and validated high-level 'as is' (not 'should be' or 'could be') stakeholder process map?
<--- Score

128. Has the improvement team collected the 'voice of the customer' (obtained feedback – qualitative and quantitative)?
<--- Score

129. What critical content must be communicated – who, what, when, where, and how?
<--- Score

130. What sort of initial information to gather?
<--- Score

131. What defines best in class?
<--- Score

132. What are the dynamics of the communication plan?
<--- Score

133. How do you hand over data centric audit context?
<--- Score

134. Who is gathering data centric audit information?
<--- Score

135. Have specific policy objectives been defined?
<--- Score

Add up total points for this section:

_____ = Total points for this section

Divided by: _____ (number of
statements answered) = _____
Average score for this section

Transfer your score to the data centric
audit Index at the beginning of the
Self-Assessment.

CRITERION #3: MEASURE:

INTENT: Gather the correct data. Measure the current performance and evolution of the situation.

In my belief, the answer to this question is clearly defined:

5 Strongly Agree

4 Agree

3 Neutral

2 Disagree

1 Strongly Disagree

1. How do you verify your resources?
<--- Score

2. What is the cost of rework?
<--- Score

3. What is the data centric audit business impact?
<--- Score

4. What details are required of the data centric audit cost structure?
<--- Score

5. Was a business case (cost/benefit) developed?
<--- Score

6. Which data centric audit impacts are significant?
<--- Score

7. What are your operating costs?
<--- Score

8. Are data centric audit vulnerabilities categorized and prioritized?
<--- Score

9. What are hidden data centric audit quality costs?
<--- Score

10. How much does it cost?
<--- Score

11. What could cause you to change course?
<--- Score

12. What does a Test Case verify?
<--- Score

13. Are you aware of what could cause a problem?
<--- Score

14. What would be a real cause for concern?
<--- Score

15. Are there measurements based on task

performance?
<--- Score

16. How can you measure the performance?
<--- Score

17. Who pays the cost?
<--- Score

18. What measurements are being captured?
<--- Score

19. What users will be impacted?
<--- Score

20. How can you measure data centric audit in a systematic way?
<--- Score

21. How do you aggregate measures across priorities?
<--- Score

22. How are costs allocated?
<--- Score

23. How do you control the overall costs of your work processes?
<--- Score

24. What measurements are possible, practicable and meaningful?
<--- Score

25. How are measurements made?
<--- Score

26. Are you taking your company in the direction of better and revenue or cheaper and cost?
<--- Score

27. What is the root cause(s) of the problem?
<--- Score

28. What are the estimated costs of proposed changes?
<--- Score

29. Are there competing data centric audit priorities?
<--- Score

30. How do your measurements capture actionable data centric audit information for use in exceeding your customers expectations and securing your customers engagement?
<--- Score

31. How can a data centric audit test verify your ideas or assumptions?
<--- Score

32. How frequently do you verify your data centric audit strategy?
<--- Score

33. How is progress measured?
<--- Score

34. How will you measure your data centric audit effectiveness?
<--- Score

35. At what cost?

<--- Score

36. What potential environmental factors impact the data centric audit effort?
<--- Score

37. How is performance measured?
<--- Score

38. Are the measurements objective?
<--- Score

39. What are the costs?
<--- Score

40. What are the data centric audit investment costs?
<--- Score

41. How will effects be measured?
<--- Score

42. What are the operational costs after data centric audit deployment?
<--- Score

43. What does losing customers cost your organization?
<--- Score

44. How do you verify performance?
<--- Score

45. Does the data centric audit task fit the client's priorities?
<--- Score

46. How will success or failure be measured?
<--- Score

47. When are costs are incurred?
<--- Score

48. What do people want to verify?
<--- Score

49. Will data centric audit have an impact on current business continuity, disaster recovery processes and/or infrastructure?
<--- Score

50. What does verifying compliance entail?
<--- Score

51. How do you verify and develop ideas and innovations?
<--- Score

52. What are your primary costs, revenues, assets?
<--- Score

53. Does management have the right priorities among projects?
<--- Score

54. How to cause the change?
<--- Score

55. Have you made assumptions about the shape of the future, particularly its impact on your customers and competitors?
<--- Score

56. Which measures and indicators matter?
<--- Score

57. What are allowable costs?
<--- Score

58. How do you measure variability?
<--- Score

59. Are supply costs steady or fluctuating?
<--- Score

60. Do you verify that corrective actions were taken?
<--- Score

61. What is the total cost related to deploying data centric audit, including any consulting or professional services?
<--- Score

62. Do you have an issue in getting priority?
<--- Score

63. What disadvantage does this cause for the user?
<--- Score

64. How will you measure success?
<--- Score

65. What is the cause of any data centric audit gaps?
<--- Score

66. What are the uncertainties surrounding estimates of impact?

<--- Score

67. What causes innovation to fail or succeed in your organization?
<--- Score

68. What relevant entities could be measured?
<--- Score

69. How frequently do you track data centric audit measures?
<--- Score

70. What is the total fixed cost?
<--- Score

71. The approach of traditional data centric audit works for detail complexity but is focused on a systematic approach rather than an understanding of the nature of systems themselves, what approach will permit your organization to deal with the kind of unpredictable emergent behaviors that dynamic complexity can introduce?
<--- Score

72. How do you stay flexible and focused to recognize larger data centric audit results?
<--- Score

73. Are actual costs in line with budgeted costs?
<--- Score

74. How do you focus on what is right -not who is right?
<--- Score

75. What are the costs and benefits?
<--- Score

76. Do you effectively measure and reward individual and team performance?
<--- Score

77. Are you able to realize any cost savings?
<--- Score

78. Did you tackle the cause or the symptom?
<--- Score

79. Why do you expend time and effort to implement measurement, for whom?
<--- Score

80. What are the types and number of measures to use?
<--- Score

81. How can you reduce costs?
<--- Score

82. What causes investor action?
<--- Score

83. Are indirect costs charged to the data centric audit program?
<--- Score

84. Where is it measured?
<--- Score

85. Which costs should be taken into account?
<--- Score

86. What drives O&M cost?
<--- Score

87. Who should receive measurement reports?
<--- Score

88. Are there any easy-to-implement alternatives to data centric audit? Sometimes other solutions are available that do not require the cost implications of a full-blown project?
<--- Score

89. Has a cost center been established?
<--- Score

90. What methods are feasible and acceptable to estimate the impact of reforms?
<--- Score

91. Is there an opportunity to verify requirements?
<--- Score

92. Where can you go to verify the info?
<--- Score

93. How do you measure efficient delivery of data centric audit services?
<--- Score

94. How will measures be used to manage and adapt?
<--- Score

95. How will your organization measure success?
<--- Score

96. How will costs be allocated?

<--- Score

97. What are the data centric audit key cost drivers?

<--- Score

98. Is the cost worth the data centric audit effort ?

<--- Score

99. What is measured? Why?

<--- Score

100. Is it possible to estimate the impact of unanticipated complexity such as wrong or failed assumptions, feedback, etcetera on proposed reforms?

<--- Score

101. What causes mismanagement?

<--- Score

102. Are missed data centric audit opportunities costing your organization money?

<--- Score

103. What are you verifying?

<--- Score

104. What tests verify requirements?

<--- Score

105. Have design-to-cost goals been established?

<--- Score

106. Do the benefits outweigh the costs?

<--- Score

107. How do you quantify and qualify impacts?
<--- Score

108. What could cause delays in the schedule?
<--- Score

109. Why a data centric audit focus?
<--- Score

110. When a disaster occurs, who gets priority?
<--- Score

111. Who is involved in verifying compliance?
<--- Score

112. What are your key data centric audit organizational performance measures, including key short and longer-term financial measures?
<--- Score

113. What do you measure and why?
<--- Score

114. Do you have any cost data centric audit limitation requirements?
<--- Score

115. How do you prevent mis-estimating cost?
<--- Score

116. How do you verify the authenticity of the data and information used?
<--- Score

117. How can you reduce the costs of obtaining

inputs?

<--- Score

118. What are the current costs of the data centric audit process?

<--- Score

119. What does your operating model cost?

<--- Score

120. Have you included everything in your data centric audit cost models?

<--- Score

121. Is the solution cost-effective?

<--- Score

122. Are the data centric audit benefits worth its costs?

<--- Score

123. Where is the cost?

<--- Score

124. How do you measure lifecycle phases?

<--- Score

125. What are your customers expectations and measures?

<--- Score

126. How do you verify if data centric audit is built right?

<--- Score

127. How do you measure success?

<--- Score

128. What can be used to verify compliance?
<--- Score

129. How do you verify and validate the data centric audit data?
<--- Score

130. What are the costs of reform?
<--- Score

131. What are the costs of delaying data centric audit action?
<--- Score

132. What evidence is there and what is measured?
<--- Score

133. Why do the measurements/indicators matter?
<--- Score

134. Among the data centric audit product and service cost to be estimated, which is considered hardest to estimate?
<--- Score

135. What are the strategic priorities for this year?
<--- Score

136. What is an unallowable cost?
<--- Score

137. What is your data centric audit quality cost segregation study?
<--- Score

138. How is the value delivered by data centric audit being measured?
<--- Score

139. How are you verifying it?
<--- Score

Add up total points for this section:
_____ = Total points for this section

Divided by: _____ (number of
statements answered) = _____
Average score for this section

Transfer your score to the data centric
audit Index at the beginning of the
Self-Assessment.

CRITERION #4: ANALYZE:

INTENT: Analyze causes, assumptions and hypotheses.

In my belief, the answer to this question is clearly defined:

5 Strongly Agree

4 Agree

3 Neutral

2 Disagree

1 Strongly Disagree

1. How was the detailed process map generated, verified, and validated?
<--- Score

2. Is the performance gap determined?
<--- Score

3. Has an output goal been set?
<--- Score

4. How will the change process be managed?
<--- Score

5. What qualifications are needed?
<--- Score

6. What quality tools were used to get through the analyze phase?
<--- Score

7. What do you need to qualify?
<--- Score

8. How do your work systems and key work processes relate to and capitalize on your core competencies?
<--- Score

9. What are your current levels and trends in key data centric audit measures or indicators of product and process performance that are important to and directly serve your customers?
<--- Score

10. How is the way you as the leader think and process information affecting your organizational culture?
<--- Score

11. Do your leaders quickly bounce back from setbacks?
<--- Score

12. Is the final output clearly identified?
<--- Score

13. What are the best opportunities for value improvement?

<--- Score

14. An organizationally feasible system request is one that considers the mission, goals and objectives of the organization, key questions are: is the data centric audit solution request practical and will it solve a problem or take advantage of an opportunity to achieve company goals?
<--- Score

15. Is there a strict change management process?
<--- Score

16. What does the data say about the performance of the stakeholder process?
<--- Score

17. What controls do you have in place to protect data?
<--- Score

18. What, related to, data centric audit processes does your organization outsource?
<--- Score

19. What did the team gain from developing a sub-process map?
<--- Score

20. What are your best practices for minimizing data centric audit project risk, while demonstrating incremental value and quick wins throughout the data centric audit project lifecycle?
<--- Score

21. How do mission and objectives affect the data

centric audit processes of your organization?

<--- Score

22. Who owns what data?

<--- Score

23. How is the data centric audit Value Stream Mapping managed?

<--- Score

24. Where is data centric audit data gathered?

<--- Score

25. Do you understand your management processes today?

<--- Score

26. Are you missing data centric audit opportunities?

<--- Score

27. What other jobs or tasks affect the performance of the steps in the data centric audit process?

<--- Score

28. What is the Value Stream Mapping?

<--- Score

29. Where can you get qualified talent today?

<--- Score

30. What is the oversight process?

<--- Score

31. What qualifications are necessary?

<--- Score

32. How do you define collaboration and team output?
<--- Score

33. Who will facilitate the team and process?
<--- Score

34. Were any designed experiments used to generate additional insight into the data analysis?
<--- Score

35. What is your organizations system for selecting qualified vendors?
<--- Score

36. What is your organizations process which leads to recognition of value generation?
<--- Score

37. What tools were used to narrow the list of possible causes?
<--- Score

38. Record-keeping requirements flow from the records needed as inputs, outputs, controls and for transformation of a data centric audit process, are the records needed as inputs to the data centric audit process available?
<--- Score

39. What are your data centric audit processes?
<--- Score

40. Think about some of the processes you undertake

within your organization, which do you own?
<--- Score

41. How are outputs preserved and protected?
<--- Score

42. Who is involved with workflow mapping?
<--- Score

43. Where is the data coming from to measure compliance?
<--- Score

44. How does the organization define, manage, and improve its data centric audit processes?
<--- Score

45. How much data can be collected in the given timeframe?
<--- Score

46. What data centric audit metrics are outputs of the process?
<--- Score

47. What are the data centric audit business drivers?
<--- Score

48. What qualifies as competition?
<--- Score

49. Who gets your output?
<--- Score

50. Has data output been validated?
<--- Score

51. Have you defined which data is gathered how?
<--- Score

52. How will the data be checked for quality?
<--- Score

53. Do your employees have the opportunity to do what they do best everyday?
<--- Score

54. What are your current levels and trends in key measures or indicators of data centric audit product and process performance that are important to and directly serve your customers? How do these results compare with the performance of your competitors and other organizations with similar offerings?
<--- Score

55. Was a cause-and-effect diagram used to explore the different types of causes (or sources of variation)?
<--- Score

56. What resources go in to get the desired output?
<--- Score

57. Are all team members qualified for all tasks?
<--- Score

58. What data do you need to collect?
<--- Score

59. What qualifications and skills do you need?
<--- Score

60. What tools were used to generate the list of

possible causes?
<--- Score

61. What were the financial benefits resulting from any 'ground fruit or low-hanging fruit' (quick fixes)?
<--- Score

62. How has the data centric audit data been gathered?
<--- Score

63. Are gaps between current performance and the goal performance identified?
<--- Score

64. What were the crucial 'moments of truth' on the process map?
<--- Score

65. What are the necessary qualifications?
<--- Score

66. What process improvements will be needed?
<--- Score

67. What output to create?
<--- Score

68. What are the disruptive data centric audit technologies that enable your organization to radically change your business processes?
<--- Score

69. Are data centric audit changes recognized early enough to be approved through the regular process?
<--- Score

70. How is data centric audit data gathered?
<--- Score

71. How will the data centric audit data be captured?
<--- Score

72. What data centric audit data will be collected?
<--- Score

73. How many input/output points does it require?
<--- Score

74. How do you measure the operational performance of your key work systems and processes, including productivity, cycle time, and other appropriate measures of process effectiveness, efficiency, and innovation?
<--- Score

75. Is the data centric audit process severely broken such that a re-design is necessary?
<--- Score

76. What information qualified as important?
<--- Score

77. What conclusions were drawn from the team's data collection and analysis? How did the team reach these conclusions?
<--- Score

78. Do several people in different organizational units assist with the data centric audit process?
<--- Score

79. Who qualifies to gain access to data?
<--- Score

80. What are the processes for audit reporting and management?
<--- Score

81. What kind of crime could a potential new hire have committed that would not only not disqualify him/her from being hired by your organization, but would actually indicate that he/she might be a particularly good fit?
<--- Score

82. What are evaluation criteria for the output?
<--- Score

83. Is the suppliers process defined and controlled?
<--- Score

84. What methods do you use to gather data centric audit data?
<--- Score

85. How do you promote understanding that opportunity for improvement is not criticism of the status quo, or the people who created the status quo?
<--- Score

86. Identify an operational issue in your organization, for example, could a particular task be done more quickly or more efficiently by data centric audit?
<--- Score

87. Is there an established change management

process?

<--- Score

88. A compounding model resolution with available relevant data can often provide insight towards a solution methodology; which data centric audit models, tools and techniques are necessary?

<--- Score

89. Who is involved in the management review process?

<--- Score

90. What data centric audit data do you gather or use now?

<--- Score

91. How do you implement and manage your work processes to ensure that they meet design requirements?

<--- Score

92. What will drive data centric audit change?

<--- Score

93. What are your key performance measures or indicators and in-process measures for the control and improvement of your data centric audit processes?

<--- Score

94. How do you ensure that the data centric audit opportunity is realistic?

<--- Score

95. Are all staff in core data centric audit subjects

Highly Qualified?
<--- Score

96. What is the data centric audit Driver?
<--- Score

97. Are your outputs consistent?
<--- Score

98. What is the output?
<--- Score

99. Is the gap/opportunity displayed and communicated in financial terms?
<--- Score

100. What is the cost of poor quality as supported by the team's analysis?
<--- Score

101. What is the complexity of the output produced?
<--- Score

102. Have the problem and goal statements been updated to reflect the additional knowledge gained from the analyze phase?
<--- Score

103. How can risk management be tied procedurally to process elements?
<--- Score

104. How difficult is it to qualify what data centric audit ROI is?
<--- Score

105. Was a detailed process map created to amplify critical steps of the 'as is' stakeholder process?
<--- Score

106. Were Pareto charts (or similar) used to portray the 'heavy hitters' (or key sources of variation)?
<--- Score

107. What types of data do your data centric audit indicators require?
<--- Score

108. What systems/processes must you excel at?
<--- Score

109. Do you have the authority to produce the output?
<--- Score

110. Should you invest in industry-recognized qualifications?
<--- Score

111. Do quality systems drive continuous improvement?
<--- Score

112. What process should you select for improvement?
<--- Score

113. Were there any improvement opportunities identified from the process analysis?
<--- Score

114. Is data and process analysis, root cause analysis

and quantifying the gap/opportunity in place?
<--- Score

115. Did any additional data need to be collected?
<--- Score

116. Is the required data centric audit data gathered?
<--- Score

117. Did any value-added analysis or 'lean thinking' take place to identify some of the gaps shown on the 'as is' process map?
<--- Score

118. Is there any way to speed up the process?
<--- Score

119. What are your outputs?
<--- Score

120. What training and qualifications will you need?
<--- Score

121. Think about the functions involved in your data centric audit project, what processes flow from these functions?
<--- Score

122. What are the personnel training and qualifications required?
<--- Score

123. What internal processes need improvement?
<--- Score

124. Have any additional benefits been identified that will result from closing all or most of the gaps?
<--- Score

125. Is pre-qualification of suppliers carried out?
<--- Score

126. What successful thing are you doing today that may be blinding you to new growth opportunities?
<--- Score

127. How is data used for program management and improvement?
<--- Score

128. How is the data gathered?
<--- Score

129. What are the revised rough estimates of the financial savings/opportunity for data centric audit improvements?
<--- Score

130. Which data centric audit data should be retained?
<--- Score

131. What data is gathered?
<--- Score

132. What data centric audit data should be collected?
<--- Score

Add up total points for this section:
_ _ _ _ _ = Total points for this section

Divided by: _____ (number of
statements answered) = _____
Average score for this section

Transfer your score to the data centric
audit Index at the beginning of the
Self-Assessment.

CRITERION #5: IMPROVE:

INTENT: Develop a practical solution. Innovate, establish and test the solution and to measure the results.

In my belief, the answer to this question is clearly defined:

5 Strongly Agree

4 Agree

3 Neutral

2 Disagree

1 Strongly Disagree

1. How are data centric audit risks managed?
<--- Score

2. Have you achieved data centric audit improvements?
<--- Score

3. Does a good decision guarantee a good outcome?

<--- Score

4. Who do you report data centric audit results to?
<--- Score

5. Who controls key decisions that will be made?
<--- Score

6. Are events managed to resolution?
<--- Score

7. Can you identify any significant risks or exposures to data centric audit third- parties (vendors, service providers, alliance partners etc) that concern you?
<--- Score

8. Who will be responsible for making the decisions to include or exclude requested changes once data centric audit is underway?
<--- Score

9. Who controls the risk?
<--- Score

10. Explorations of the frontiers of data centric audit will help you build influence, improve data centric audit, optimize decision making, and sustain change, what is your approach?
<--- Score

11. What were the criteria for evaluating a data centric audit pilot?
<--- Score

12. What can you do to improve?

<--- Score

13. How do you keep improving data centric audit?
<--- Score

14. Are the most efficient solutions problem-specific?
<--- Score

15. What is data centric audit risk?
<--- Score

16. What are the expected data centric audit results?
<--- Score

17. Is there a high likelihood that any recommendations will achieve their intended results?
<--- Score

18. What should a proof of concept or pilot accomplish?
<--- Score

19. Was a data centric audit charter developed?
<--- Score

20. data centric audit risk decisions: whose call Is It?
<--- Score

21. What data centric audit improvements can be made?
<--- Score

22. Will the controls trigger any other risks?
<--- Score

23. Who are the data centric audit decision-makers?
<--- Score

24. Can the solution be designed and implemented within an acceptable time period?
<--- Score

25. Is the data centric audit risk managed?
<--- Score

26. How will you recognize and celebrate results?
<--- Score

27. What actually has to improve and by how much?
<--- Score

28. Why improve in the first place?
<--- Score

29. How can skill-level changes improve data centric audit?
<--- Score

30. What is the data centric audit's sustainability risk?
<--- Score

31. What lessons, if any, from a pilot were incorporated into the design of the full-scale solution?
<--- Score

32. Is the solution technically practical?
<--- Score

33. What assumptions are made about the solution and approach?

<--- Score

34. Is the data centric audit documentation thorough?
<--- Score

35. Is the measure of success for data centric audit understandable to a variety of people?
<--- Score

36. What is the team's contingency plan for potential problems occurring in implementation?
<--- Score

37. Which data centric audit solution is appropriate?
<--- Score

38. What tools do you use once you have decided on a data centric audit strategy and more importantly how do you choose?
<--- Score

39. Have you identified breakpoints and/or risk tolerances that will trigger broad consideration of a potential need for intervention or modification of strategy?
<--- Score

40. What are your current levels and trends in key measures or indicators of workforce and leader development?
<--- Score

41. Are the key business and technology risks being managed?
<--- Score

42. How do you measure progress and evaluate training effectiveness?

<--- Score

43. What is data centric audit's impact on utilizing the best solution(s)?

<--- Score

44. Would you develop a data centric audit Communication Strategy?

<--- Score

45. How do you improve your likelihood of success ?

<--- Score

46. How do you go about comparing data centric audit approaches/solutions?

<--- Score

47. Are risk triggers captured?

<--- Score

48. What are the concrete data centric audit results?

<--- Score

49. What improvements have been achieved?

<--- Score

50. How risky is your organization?

<--- Score

51. What do you want to improve?

<--- Score

52. How can the phases of data centric audit development be identified?
<--- Score

53. Are decisions made in a timely manner?
<--- Score

54. How does your organization evaluate strategic data centric audit success?
<--- Score

55. If you could go back in time five years, what decision would you make differently? What is your best guess as to what decision you're making today you might regret five years from now?
<--- Score

56. How will you know when its improved?
<--- Score

57. Is any data centric audit documentation required?
<--- Score

58. What strategies for data centric audit improvement are successful?
<--- Score

59. Is risk periodically assessed?
<--- Score

60. Risk Identification: What are the possible risk events your organization faces in relation to data centric audit?
<--- Score

61. Who are the people involved in developing and

implementing data centric audit?

<--- Score

62. How do you link measurement and risk?

<--- Score

63. What communications are necessary to support the implementation of the solution?

<--- Score

64. Can you integrate quality management and risk management?

<--- Score

65. Who will be using the results of the measurement activities?

<--- Score

66. Do vendor agreements bring new compliance risk ?

<--- Score

67. Where do you need data centric audit improvement?

<--- Score

68. How do the data centric audit results compare with the performance of your competitors and other organizations with similar offerings?

<--- Score

69. What is the risk?

<--- Score

70. Where do the data centric audit decisions reside?

<--- Score

71. Do those selected for the data centric audit team have a good general understanding of what data centric audit is all about?
<--- Score

72. For estimation problems, how do you develop an estimation statement?
<--- Score

73. How can you improve data centric audit?
<--- Score

74. How does the team improve its work?
<--- Score

75. Do you need to do a usability evaluation?
<--- Score

76. What alternative responses are available to manage risk?
<--- Score

77. Who manages supplier risk management in your organization?
<--- Score

78. How do you mitigate data centric audit risk?
<--- Score

79. What practices helps your organization to develop its capacity to recognize patterns?
<--- Score

80. What is the implementation plan?
<--- Score

81. Is supporting data centric audit documentation required?
<--- Score

82. How can you better manage risk?
<--- Score

83. Are procedures documented for managing data centric audit risks?
<--- Score

84. What is your decision requirements diagram?
<--- Score

85. How do you measure improved data centric audit service perception, and satisfaction?
<--- Score

86. At what point will vulnerability assessments be performed once data centric audit is put into production (e.g., ongoing Risk Management after implementation)?
<--- Score

87. Are the risks fully understood, reasonable and manageable?
<--- Score

88. How is knowledge sharing about risk management improved?
<--- Score

89. What error proofing will be done to address some of the discrepancies observed in the 'as is' process?
<--- Score

90. Who are the key stakeholders for the data centric audit evaluation?

<--- Score

91. How do you decide how much to remunerate an employee?

<--- Score

92. What are the affordable data centric audit risks?

<--- Score

93. How can you improve performance?

<--- Score

94. What area needs the greatest improvement?

<--- Score

95. In the past few months, what is the smallest change you have made that has had the biggest positive result? What was it about that small change that produced the large return?

<--- Score

96. How do you improve data centric audit service perception, and satisfaction?

<--- Score

97. What needs improvement? Why?

<--- Score

98. What were the underlying assumptions on the cost-benefit analysis?

<--- Score

99. How do you deal with data centric audit risk?
<--- Score

100. What tools were used to tap into the creativity and encourage 'outside the box' thinking?
<--- Score

101. What are the implications of the one critical data centric audit decision 10 minutes, 10 months, and 10 years from now?
<--- Score

102. How do you define the solutions' scope?
<--- Score

103. What attendant changes will need to be made to ensure that the solution is successful?
<--- Score

104. Is the data centric audit solution sustainable?
<--- Score

105. Does the goal represent a desired result that can be measured?
<--- Score

106. How will you know that a change is an improvement?
<--- Score

107. Who will be responsible for documenting the data centric audit requirements in detail?
<--- Score

108. How will you know that you have improved?
<--- Score

109. Who should make the data centric audit decisions?

<--- Score

110. Is there any other data centric audit solution?

<--- Score

111. Risk factors: what are the characteristics of data centric audit that make it risky?

<--- Score

112. What resources are required for the improvement efforts?

<--- Score

113. How do you manage and improve your data centric audit work systems to deliver customer value and achieve organizational success and sustainability?

<--- Score

114. What current systems have to be understood and/or changed?

<--- Score

115. Are you assessing data centric audit and risk?

<--- Score

116. How do you measure risk?

<--- Score

117. Risk events: what are the things that could go wrong?

<--- Score

118. What tools were most useful during the improve phase?
<--- Score

119. What went well, what should change, what can improve?
<--- Score

120. How do you improve productivity?
<--- Score

121. What tools were used to evaluate the potential solutions?
<--- Score

122. How are policy decisions made and where?
<--- Score

123. For decision problems, how do you develop a decision statement?
<--- Score

124. What does the 'should be' process map/design look like?
<--- Score

125. When you map the key players in your own work and the types/domains of relationships with them, which relationships do you find easy and which challenging, and why?
<--- Score

126. How significant is the improvement in the eyes of the end user?
<--- Score

127. How scalable is your data centric audit solution?
<--- Score

128. Who makes the data centric audit decisions in your organization?
<--- Score

129. Who manages data centric audit risk?
<--- Score

130. What to do with the results or outcomes of measurements?
<--- Score

Add up total points for this section:
_ _ _ _ _ = Total points for this section

Divided by: _ _ _ _ _ _ (number of statements answered) = _ _ _ _ _ _
Average score for this section

Transfer your score to the data centric audit Index at the beginning of the Self-Assessment.

CRITERION #6: CONTROL:

INTENT: Implement the practical solution. Maintain the performance and correct possible complications.

In my belief, the answer to this question is clearly defined:

5 Strongly Agree

4 Agree

3 Neutral

2 Disagree

1 Strongly Disagree

1. In the case of a data centric audit project, the criteria for the audit derive from implementation objectives, an audit of a data centric audit project involves assessing whether the recommendations outlined for implementation have been met, can you track that any data centric audit project is implemented as planned, and is it working?
<--- Score

2. Where do ideas that reach policy makers and planners as proposals for data centric audit strengthening and reform actually originate?
<--- Score

3. What is your theory of human motivation, and how does your compensation plan fit with that view?
<--- Score

4. Is there a data centric audit Communication plan covering who needs to get what information when?
<--- Score

5. What do you stand for--and what are you against?
<--- Score

6. Has the improved process and its steps been standardized?
<--- Score

7. How do your controls stack up?
<--- Score

8. What are the known security controls?
<--- Score

9. What should the next improvement project be that is related to data centric audit?
<--- Score

10. What can you control?
<--- Score

11. Act/Adjust: What Do you Need to Do Differently?
<--- Score

12. What is the control/monitoring plan?
<--- Score

13. Is a response plan established and deployed?
<--- Score

14. Are controls in place and consistently applied?
<--- Score

15. Is there a control plan in place for sustaining improvements (short and long-term)?
<--- Score

16. Is there a documented and implemented monitoring plan?
<--- Score

17. Does job training on the documented procedures need to be part of the process team's education and training?
<--- Score

18. Is the data centric audit test/monitoring cost justified?
<--- Score

19. What do your reports reflect?
<--- Score

20. Implementation Planning: is a pilot needed to test the changes before a full roll out occurs?
<--- Score

21. How do you monitor usage and cost?
<--- Score

22. How do you plan for the cost of succession?
<--- Score

23. You may have created your quality measures at a time when you lacked resources, technology wasn't up to the required standard, or low service levels were the industry norm. Have those circumstances changed?
<--- Score

24. What are you attempting to measure/monitor?
<--- Score

25. How will the process owner and team be able to hold the gains?
<--- Score

26. Are there documented procedures?
<--- Score

27. Does the data centric audit performance meet the customer's requirements?
<--- Score

28. How widespread is its use?
<--- Score

29. Are operating procedures consistent?
<--- Score

30. Can support from partners be adjusted?
<--- Score

31. Is there a standardized process?
<--- Score

32. How do controls support value?
<--- Score

33. Who sets the data centric audit standards?
<--- Score

34. How do senior leaders actions reflect a commitment to the organizations data centric audit values?
<--- Score

35. How do you establish and deploy modified action plans if circumstances require a shift in plans and rapid execution of new plans?
<--- Score

36. Are the planned controls in place?
<--- Score

37. Is there documentation that will support the successful operation of the improvement?
<--- Score

38. What other areas of the group might benefit from the data centric audit team's improvements, knowledge, and learning?
<--- Score

39. How will the day-to-day responsibilities for monitoring and continual improvement be transferred from the improvement team to the process owner?
<--- Score

40. Is there a recommended audit plan for routine surveillance inspections of data centric audit's gains?

<--- Score

41. How will input, process, and output variables be checked to detect for sub-optimal conditions?
<--- Score

42. Do the data centric audit decisions you make today help people and the planet tomorrow?
<--- Score

43. Are the data centric audit standards challenging?
<--- Score

44. What are the critical parameters to watch?
<--- Score

45. Will your goals reflect your program budget?
<--- Score

46. What is your plan to assess your security risks?
<--- Score

47. What other systems, operations, processes, and infrastructures (hiring practices, staffing, training, incentives/rewards, metrics/dashboards/scorecards, etc.) need updates, additions, changes, or deletions in order to facilitate knowledge transfer and improvements?
<--- Score

48. How will report readings be checked to effectively monitor performance?
<--- Score

49. What are the key elements of your data centric audit performance improvement system, including

your evaluation, organizational learning, and innovation processes?

<--- Score

50. Do you monitor the effectiveness of your data centric audit activities?

<--- Score

51. How can you best use all of your knowledge repositories to enhance learning and sharing?

<--- Score

52. Does data centric audit appropriately measure and monitor risk?

<--- Score

53. Are documented procedures clear and easy to follow for the operators?

<--- Score

54. Will the team be available to assist members in planning investigations?

<--- Score

55. Do you monitor the data centric audit decisions made and fine tune them as they evolve?

<--- Score

56. What quality tools were useful in the control phase?

<--- Score

57. How do you plan on providing proper recognition and disclosure of supporting companies?

<--- Score

58. What adjustments to the strategies are needed?
<--- Score

59. How might the group capture best practices and lessons learned so as to leverage improvements?
<--- Score

60. How will new or emerging customer needs/requirements be checked/communicated to orient the process toward meeting the new specifications and continually reducing variation?
<--- Score

61. Is there an action plan in case of emergencies?
<--- Score

62. Are the planned controls working?
<--- Score

63. Will any special training be provided for results interpretation?
<--- Score

64. Are pertinent alerts monitored, analyzed and distributed to appropriate personnel?
<--- Score

65. Does the response plan contain a definite closed loop continual improvement scheme (e.g., plan-do-check-act)?
<--- Score

66. Is a response plan in place for when the input, process, or output measures indicate an 'out-of-control' condition?
<--- Score

67. Is reporting being used or needed?
<--- Score

68. Is new knowledge gained imbedded in the response plan?
<--- Score

69. How likely is the current data centric audit plan to come in on schedule or on budget?
<--- Score

70. Who will be in control?
<--- Score

71. What is the recommended frequency of auditing?
<--- Score

72. What should you measure to verify efficiency gains?
<--- Score

73. What are your results for key measures or indicators of the accomplishment of your data centric audit strategy and action plans, including building and strengthening core competencies?
<--- Score

74. How is data centric audit project cost planned, managed, monitored?
<--- Score

75. Does a troubleshooting guide exist or is it needed?
<--- Score

76. Has the data centric audit value of standards been

quantified?

<--- Score

77. Who controls critical resources?

<--- Score

78. Against what alternative is success being
measured?

<--- Score

79. Who is the data centric audit process owner?

<--- Score

80. How do you spread information?

<--- Score

81. Is knowledge gained on process shared and
institutionalized?

<--- Score

82. What are customers monitoring?

<--- Score

83. Are you measuring, monitoring and predicting
data centric audit activities to optimize operations
and profitability, and enhancing outcomes?

<--- Score

84. What do you measure to verify effectiveness
gains?

<--- Score

85. Are suggested corrective/restorative actions
indicated on the response plan for known causes to
problems that might surface?

<--- Score

86. Who has control over resources?
<--- Score

87. How will you measure your QA plan's effectiveness?
<--- Score

88. Are new process steps, standards, and documentation ingrained into normal operations?
<--- Score

89. Who is going to spread your message?
<--- Score

90. How do you encourage people to take control and responsibility?
<--- Score

91. How will the process owner verify improvement in present and future sigma levels, process capabilities?
<--- Score

92. How is change control managed?
<--- Score

93. What is the best design framework for data centric audit organization now that, in a post industrial-age if the top-down, command and control model is no longer relevant?
<--- Score

94. Is there a transfer of ownership and knowledge to process owner and process team tasked with the responsibilities.
<--- Score

95. What key inputs and outputs are being measured on an ongoing basis?
<--- Score

96. Have new or revised work instructions resulted?
<--- Score

97. How will data centric audit decisions be made and monitored?
<--- Score

Add up total points for this section:
_____ = Total points for this section

Divided by: _____ (number of statements answered) = _____
Average score for this section

Transfer your score to the data centric audit Index at the beginning of the Self-Assessment.

CRITERION #7: SUSTAIN:

INTENT: Retain the benefits.

In my belief, the answer to this question is clearly defined:

5 Strongly Agree

4 Agree

3 Neutral

2 Disagree

1 Strongly Disagree

1. Is data centric audit dependent on the successful delivery of a current project?
<--- Score

2. Is data centric audit realistic, or are you setting yourself up for failure?
<--- Score

3. What goals did you miss?
<--- Score

4. What are your personal philosophies regarding data centric audit and how do they influence your work?
<--- Score

5. How do you set data centric audit stretch targets and how do you get people to not only participate in setting these stretch targets but also that they strive to achieve these?
<--- Score

6. Have new benefits been realized?
<--- Score

7. Who are four people whose careers you have enhanced?
<--- Score

8. How will you motivate the stakeholders with the least vested interest?
<--- Score

9. Is it economical; do you have the time and money?
<--- Score

10. Who will manage the integration of tools?
<--- Score

11. Instead of going to current contacts for new ideas, what if you reconnected with dormant contacts-- the people you used to know? If you were going reactivate a dormant tie, who would it be?
<--- Score

12. Who is responsible for errors?
<--- Score

13. Which functions and people interact with the supplier and or customer?
<--- Score

14. Do you have the right people on the bus?
<--- Score

15. How do you track customer value, profitability or financial return, organizational success, and sustainability?
<--- Score

16. How do you keep records, of what?
<--- Score

17. Who have you, as a company, historically been when you've been at your best?
<--- Score

18. If you were responsible for initiating and implementing major changes in your organization, what steps might you take to ensure acceptance of those changes?
<--- Score

19. When information truly is ubiquitous, when reach and connectivity are completely global, when computing resources are infinite, and when a whole new set of impossibilities are not only possible, but happening, what will that do to your business?
<--- Score

20. Is a data centric audit team work effort in place?
<--- Score

21. Are the assumptions believable and achievable?
<--- Score

22. Think of your data centric audit project, what are the main functions?
<--- Score

23. What is your BATNA (best alternative to a negotiated agreement)?
<--- Score

24. Do you know who is a friend or a foe?
<--- Score

25. Are your responses positive or negative?
<--- Score

26. If your company went out of business tomorrow, would anyone who doesn't get a paycheck here care?
<--- Score

27. Is maximizing data centric audit protection the same as minimizing data centric audit loss?
<--- Score

28. What is a feasible sequencing of reform initiatives over time?
<--- Score

29. Are you satisfied with your current role? If not, what is missing from it?
<--- Score

30. Where can you break convention?

<--- Score

31. What trophy do you want on your mantle?
<--- Score

32. What are you challenging?
<--- Score

33. Can you do all this work?
<--- Score

34. Is your strategy driving your strategy? Or is the way in which you allocate resources driving your strategy?
<--- Score

35. How will you insure seamless interoperability of data centric audit moving forward?
<--- Score

36. In a project to restructure data centric audit outcomes, which stakeholders would you involve?
<--- Score

37. What projects are going on in the organization today, and what resources are those projects using from the resource pools?
<--- Score

38. Which data centric audit goals are the most important?
<--- Score

39. How will you know that the data centric audit project has been successful?
<--- Score

40. What are the challenges?
<--- Score

41. Are you relevant? Will you be relevant five years from now? Ten?
<--- Score

42. Operational - will it work?
<--- Score

43. Who is the main stakeholder, with ultimate responsibility for driving data centric audit forward?
<--- Score

44. How do you provide a safe environment -physically and emotionally?
<--- Score

45. If your customer were your grandmother, would you tell her to buy what you're selling?
<--- Score

46. What is the estimated value of the project?
<--- Score

47. What you are going to do to affect the numbers?
<--- Score

48. What are current data centric audit paradigms?
<--- Score

49. Whose voice (department, ethnic group, women, older workers, etc) might you have missed hearing from in your company, and how might you amplify

this voice to create positive momentum for your business?

<--- Score

50. How do you engage the workforce, in addition to satisfying them?

<--- Score

51. How do you cross-sell and up-sell your data centric audit success?

<--- Score

52. If you got fired and a new hire took your place, what would she do different?

<--- Score

53. Is the data centric audit organization completing tasks effectively and efficiently?

<--- Score

54. What did you miss in the interview for the worst hire you ever made?

<--- Score

55. What threat is data centric audit addressing?

<--- Score

56. What data centric audit modifications can you make work for you?

<--- Score

57. What is your competitive advantage?

<--- Score

58. Who are your customers?

<--- Score

59. What unique value proposition (UVP) do you offer?
<--- Score

60. What is your question? Why?
<--- Score

61. What is effective data centric audit?
<--- Score

62. Do you know what you are doing? And who do you call if you don't?
<--- Score

63. If you find that you havent accomplished one of the goals for one of the steps of the data centric audit strategy, what will you do to fix it?
<--- Score

64. Why should people listen to you?
<--- Score

65. What happens if you do not have enough funding?
<--- Score

66. How do you foster the skills, knowledge, talents, attributes, and characteristics you want to have?
<--- Score

67. What is the funding source for this project?
<--- Score

68. What is the big data centric audit idea?
<--- Score

69. What have you done to protect your business from competitive encroachment?
<--- Score

70. What one word do you want to own in the minds of your customers, employees, and partners?
<--- Score

71. What are the performance and scale of the data centric audit tools?
<--- Score

72. How much contingency will be available in the budget?
<--- Score

73. Do you see more potential in people than they do in themselves?
<--- Score

74. In the past year, what have you done (or could you have done) to increase the accurate perception of your company/brand as ethical and honest?
<--- Score

75. What are the short and long-term data centric audit goals?
<--- Score

76. Have benefits been optimized with all key stakeholders?
<--- Score

77. What potential megatrends could make your

business model obsolete?

<--- Score

78. What information is critical to your organization that your executives are ignoring?

<--- Score

79. Which models, tools and techniques are necessary?

<--- Score

80. How do you determine the key elements that affect data centric audit workforce satisfaction, how are these elements determined for different workforce groups and segments?

<--- Score

81. How do customers see your organization?

<--- Score

82. Do you think you know, or do you know you know ?

<--- Score

83. What are the essentials of internal data centric audit management?

<--- Score

84. If you had to leave your organization for a year and the only communication you could have with employees/colleagues was a single paragraph, what would you write?

<--- Score

85. Are you / should you be revolutionary or evolutionary?

<--- Score

86. How do you make it meaningful in connecting data centric audit with what users do day-to-day?
<--- Score

87. Do data centric audit rules make a reasonable demand on a users capabilities?
<--- Score

88. How do you go about securing data centric audit?
<--- Score

89. What are specific data centric audit rules to follow?
<--- Score

90. What would you recommend your friend do if he/she were facing this dilemma?
<--- Score

91. Do you say no to customers for no reason?
<--- Score

92. What will be the consequences to the stakeholder (financial, reputation etc) if data centric audit does not go ahead or fails to deliver the objectives?
<--- Score

93. What are strategies for increasing support and reducing opposition?
<--- Score

94. What was the last experiment you ran?
<--- Score

95. What are the usability implications of data

centric audit actions?
<--- Score

96. Are you making progress, and are you making progress as data centric audit leaders?
<--- Score

97. Can you break it down?
<--- Score

98. Which individuals, teams or departments will be involved in data centric audit?
<--- Score

99. What are the potential basics of data centric audit fraud?
<--- Score

100. What are the key enablers to make this data centric audit move?
<--- Score

101. How do you ensure that implementations of data centric audit products are done in a way that ensures safety?
<--- Score

102. Do you have past data centric audit successes?
<--- Score

103. Who is responsible for ensuring appropriate resources (time, people and money) are allocated to data centric audit?
<--- Score

104. Were lessons learned captured and

communicated?
<--- Score

105. How can you negotiate data centric audit successfully with a stubborn boss, an irate client, or a deceitful coworker?
<--- Score

106. Do you have enough freaky customers in your portfolio pushing you to the limit day in and day out?
<--- Score

107. What could happen if you do not do it?
<--- Score

108. If you had to rebuild your organization without any traditional competitive advantages (i.e., no killer technology, promising research, innovative product/ service delivery model, etcetera), how would your people have to approach their work and collaborate together in order to create the necessary conditions for success?
<--- Score

109. What must you excel at?
<--- Score

110. How can you become the company that would put you out of business?
<--- Score

111. What are the barriers to increased data centric audit production?
<--- Score

112. How do you foster innovation?
<--- Score

113. Are you changing as fast as the world around you?
<--- Score

114. What counts that you are not counting?
<--- Score

115. What is the range of capabilities?
<--- Score

116. If no one would ever find out about your accomplishments, how would you lead differently?
<--- Score

117. How do you accomplish your long range data centric audit goals?
<--- Score

118. What are internal and external data centric audit relations?
<--- Score

119. Why is it important to have senior management support for a data centric audit project?
<--- Score

120. What is the recommended frequency of auditing?
<--- Score

121. Can the schedule be done in the given time?
<--- Score

122. What relationships among data centric audit trends do you perceive?
<--- Score

123. Is your basic point _____ or _____?
<--- Score

124. Would you rather sell to knowledgeable and informed customers or to uninformed customers?
<--- Score

125. What trouble can you get into?
<--- Score

126. What is it like to work for you?
<--- Score

127. Do you have the right capabilities and capacities?
<--- Score

128. What management system can you use to leverage the data centric audit experience, ideas, and concerns of the people closest to the work to be done?
<--- Score

129. To whom do you add value?
<--- Score

130. How do senior leaders deploy your organizations vision and values through your leadership system, to the workforce, to key suppliers and partners, and to customers and other stakeholders, as appropriate?
<--- Score

131. Are all key stakeholders present at all Structured Walkthroughs?

<--- Score

132. What are the long-term data centric audit goals?

<--- Score

133. How do you keep the momentum going?

<--- Score

134. In retrospect, of the projects that you pulled the plug on, what percent do you wish had been allowed to keep going, and what percent do you wish had ended earlier?

<--- Score

135. What is the purpose of data centric audit in relation to the mission?

<--- Score

136. How do you transition from the baseline to the target?

<--- Score

137. How likely is it that a customer would recommend your company to a friend or colleague?

<--- Score

138. Who will be responsible for deciding whether data centric audit goes ahead or not after the initial investigations?

<--- Score

139. Can you maintain your growth without

detracting from the factors that have contributed to your success?
<--- Score

140. Are there any activities that you can take off your to do list?
<--- Score

141. How do you deal with data centric audit changes?
<--- Score

142. Who else should you help?
<--- Score

143. If you do not follow, then how to lead?
<--- Score

144. Are new benefits received and understood?
<--- Score

145. What is the kind of project structure that would be appropriate for your data centric audit project, should it be formal and complex, or can it be less formal and relatively simple?
<--- Score

146. What is the craziest thing you can do?
<--- Score

147. Political -is anyone trying to undermine this project?
<--- Score

148. Is a data centric audit breakthrough on the horizon?

<--- Score

149. What business benefits will data centric audit goals deliver if achieved?
<--- Score

150. How do you govern and fulfill your societal responsibilities?
<--- Score

151. What is the source of the strategies for data centric audit strengthening and reform?
<--- Score

152. What new services of functionality will be implemented next with data centric audit ?
<--- Score

153. What are the business goals data centric audit is aiming to achieve?
<--- Score

154. How do you lead with data centric audit in mind?
<--- Score

155. Why not do data centric audit?
<--- Score

156. How can you become more high-tech but still be high touch?
<--- Score

157. How will you ensure you get what you expected?
<--- Score

158. Ask yourself: how would you do this work if you only had one staff member to do it?
<--- Score

159. What is your data centric audit strategy?
<--- Score

160. At what moment would you think; Will I get fired?
<--- Score

161. Are the criteria for selecting recommendations stated?
<--- Score

162. Whom among your colleagues do you trust, and for what?
<--- Score

163. What role does communication play in the success or failure of a data centric audit project?
<--- Score

164. What are the gaps in your knowledge and experience?
<--- Score

165. What stupid rule would you most like to kill?
<--- Score

166. Who are the key stakeholders?
<--- Score

167. Are you maintaining a past–present–future perspective throughout the data centric audit discussion?
<--- Score

168. What happens at your organization when people fail?

<--- Score

169. Who is on the team?

<--- Score

170. Why is data centric audit important for you now?

<--- Score

171. What happens when a new employee joins the organization?

<--- Score

172. What may be the consequences for the performance of an organization if all stakeholders are not consulted regarding data centric audit?

<--- Score

173. What have been your experiences in defining long range data centric audit goals?

<--- Score

174. Why will customers want to buy your organizations products/services?

<--- Score

175. How is implementation research currently incorporated into each of your goals?

<--- Score

176. What is an unauthorized commitment?

<--- Score

177. Who do you think the world wants your organization to be?
<--- Score

178. Who will determine interim and final deadlines?
<--- Score

179. What data centric audit skills are most important?
<--- Score

180. What are you trying to prove to yourself, and how might it be hijacking your life and business success?
<--- Score

181. Are you using a design thinking approach and integrating Innovation, data centric audit Experience, and Brand Value?
<--- Score

182. Do you have an implicit bias for capital investments over people investments?
<--- Score

183. What are the success criteria that will indicate that data centric audit objectives have been met and the benefits delivered?
<--- Score

184. What is your formula for success in data centric audit ?
<--- Score

185. How much does data centric audit help?
<--- Score

186. How do you create buy-in?

<--- Score

187. What are the top 3 things at the forefront of your data centric audit agendas for the next 3 years?
<--- Score

188. Will there be any necessary staff changes (redundancies or new hires)?
<--- Score

189. Marketing budgets are tighter, consumers are more skeptical, and social media has changed forever the way we talk about data centric audit, how do you gain traction?
<--- Score

190. What knowledge, skills and characteristics mark a good data centric audit project manager?
<--- Score

191. How do you maintain data centric audit's Integrity?
<--- Score

192. Is there a work around that you can use?
<--- Score

193. Will it be accepted by users?
<--- Score

194. Is there any existing data centric audit governance structure?
<--- Score

195. Why should you adopt a data centric audit

framework?

<--- Score

196. How do you manage data centric audit
Knowledge Management (KM)?

<--- Score

**197. If you weren't already in this business, would
you enter it today? And if not, what are you going
to do about it?**

<--- Score

198. Do you think data centric audit accomplishes the
goals you expect it to accomplish?

<--- Score

199. What do we do when new problems arise?

<--- Score

200. How can you incorporate support to ensure
safe and effective use of data centric audit into the
services that you provide?

<--- Score

**201. How important is data centric audit to the
user organizations mission?**

<--- Score

202. How do you assess the data centric audit pitfalls
that are inherent in implementing it?

<--- Score

203. What is the overall business strategy?

<--- Score

204. Do you feel that more should be done in the data

centric audit area?
<--- Score

205. How long will it take to change?
<--- Score

206. Why do and why don't your customers like your organization?
<--- Score

207. What would have to be true for the option on the table to be the best possible choice?
<--- Score

208. Who do you want your customers to become?
<--- Score

209. What does your signature ensure?
<--- Score

210. Who do we want your customers to become?
<--- Score

211. Who is responsible for data centric audit?
<--- Score

212. What is the overall talent health of your organization as a whole at senior levels, and for each organization reporting to a member of the Senior Leadership Team?
<--- Score

213. Who will provide the final approval of data centric audit deliverables?
<--- Score

214. How do you stay inspired?
<--- Score

Add up total points for this section:
_____ = Total points for this section

Divided by: _____ (number of
statements answered) = _____
Average score for this section

Transfer your score to the data centric
audit Index at the beginning of the
Self-Assessment.

Data Centric Audit and Managing Projects, Criteria for Project Managers:

1.0 Initiating Process Group: Data Centric Audit

1. Specific - is the objective clear in terms of what, how, when, and where the situation will be changed?

2. What will be the pressing issues of tomorrow?

3. How should needs be met?

4. Do you know the roles & responsibilities required for this Data Centric Audit project?

5. Are you certain deliverables are properly completed and meet quality standards?

6. What are the required resources?

7. How can you make your needs known?

8. What must be done?

9. Based on your Data Centric Audit project communication management plan, what worked well?

10. What do you need to do?

11. The Data Centric Audit project you are managing has nine stakeholders. How many channel of communications are there between corresponding stakeholders?

12. Mitigate. what will you do to minimize the impact should the risk event occur?

13. How to control and approve each phase?

14. Were escalated issues resolved promptly?

15. When must it be done?

16. What will you do?

17. What communication items need improvement?

18. Are the changes in your Data Centric Audit project being formally requested, analyzed, and approved by the appropriate decision makers?

19. Are there resources to maintain and support the outcome of the Data Centric Audit project?

20. Who is behind the Data Centric Audit project?

1.1 Project Charter: Data Centric Audit

21. What are the deliverables?

22. Does the Data Centric Audit project need to consider any special capacity or capability issues?

23. Dependent Data Centric Audit projects: what Data Centric Audit projects must be underway or completed before this Data Centric Audit project can be successful?

24. Why is it important?

25. Must Have?

26. Is it an improvement over existing products?

27. What metrics could you look at?

28. Will this replace an existing product?

29. What is the most common tool for helping define the detail?

30. Strategic fit: what is the strategic initiative identifier for this Data Centric Audit project?

31. What are some examples of a business case?

32. Data Centric Audit project deliverables: what is the Data Centric Audit project going to produce?

33. Data Centric Audit project objective statement:

what must the Data Centric Audit project do?

34. Who manages integration?

35. Who is the sponsor?

36. When is a charter needed?

37. Did your Data Centric Audit project ask for this?

38. Success determination factors: how will the success of the Data Centric Audit project be determined from the customers perspective?

39. Run it as as a startup?

40. Why have you chosen the aim you have set forth?

1.2 Stakeholder Register: Data Centric Audit

41. What & Why?

42. What are the major Data Centric Audit project milestones requiring communications or providing communications opportunities?

43. How will reports be created?

44. What is the power of the stakeholder?

45. What opportunities exist to provide communications?

46. How much influence do they have on the Data Centric Audit project?

47. Who are the stakeholders?

48. Is your organization ready for change?

49. How big is the gap?

50. Who is managing stakeholder engagement?

51. Who wants to talk about Security?

52. How should employers make voices heard?

1.3 Stakeholder Analysis Matrix: Data Centric Audit

53. Niche target markets?

54. How can you counter negative efforts?

55. New technologies, services, ideas?

56. Benefit to whom?

57. What is accountability in relation to the Data Centric Audit project?

58. Opponents; who are the opponents?

59. Technology development and innovation?

60. Business and product development?

61. Philosophy and values?

62. Supporters; who are the supporters?

63. If the baseline is now, and if its improved it will be better than now?

64. Who will be affected by the work?

65. What is in it for you?

66. Guiding question: what is the issue at stake?

67. Geographical, export, import?

68. Sustaining internal capabilities?

69. Location and geographical?

70. New USPs?

71. Who is most dependent on the resources at stake?

2.0 Planning Process Group: Data Centric Audit

72. How does activity resource estimation affect activity duration estimation?

73. What is the NEXT thing to do?

74. What is a Software Development Life Cycle (SDLC)?

75. If task x starts two days late, what is the effect on the Data Centric Audit project end date?

76. What is involved in Data Centric Audit project scope management, and why is good Data Centric Audit project scope management so important on information technology Data Centric Audit projects?

77. What type of estimation method are you using?

78. Are there efficient coordination mechanisms to avoid overloading the counterparts, participating stakeholders?

79. Data Centric Audit project assessment; why did you do this Data Centric Audit project?

80. What is the critical path for this Data Centric Audit project, and what is the duration of the critical path?

81. What business situation is being addressed?

82. Are you just doing busywork to pass the time?

83. Explanation: is what the Data Centric Audit project intents to solve a hard question?

84. If you are late, will anybody notice?

85. First of all, should any action be taken?

86. Are the necessary foundations in place to ensure the sustainability of the results of the Data Centric Audit project?

87. How will you know you did it?

88. In which Data Centric Audit project management process group is the detailed Data Centric Audit project budget created?

89. In what way has the program contributed towards the issue culture and development included on the public agenda?

90. What types of differentiated effects are resulting from the Data Centric Audit project and to what extent?

91. How well will the chosen processes produce the expected results?

2.1 Project Management Plan: Data Centric Audit

92. Are there any windfall benefits that would accrue to the Data Centric Audit project sponsor or other parties?

93. Is the budget realistic?

94. What are the assigned resources?

95. What are the known stakeholder requirements?

96. What are the constraints?

97. What worked well?

98. Is mitigation authorized or recommended?

99. Do the proposed changes from the Data Centric Audit project include any significant risks to safety?

100. How do you manage integration?

101. Are the existing and future without-plan conditions reasonable and appropriate?

102. Is there an incremental analysis/cost effectiveness analysis of proposed mitigation features based on an approved method and using an accepted model?

103. What would you do differently what did not

work?

104. What is Data Centric Audit project scope management?

105. If the Data Centric Audit project is complex or scope is specialized, do you have appropriate and/or qualified staff available to perform the tasks?

106. Is the appropriate plan selected based on your organizations objectives and evaluation criteria expressed in Principles and Guidelines policies?

107. How do you organize the costs in the Data Centric Audit project management plan?

108. If the Data Centric Audit project management plan is a comprehensive document that guides you in Data Centric Audit project execution and control, then what should it NOT contain?

109. How well are you able to manage your risk?

2.2 Scope Management Plan: Data Centric Audit

110. Why do you need to manage scope?

111. Are Data Centric Audit project leaders committed to this Data Centric Audit project full time?

112. Are changes in deliverable commitments agreed to by all affected groups & individuals?

113. Are the quality tools and methods identified in the Quality Plan appropriate to the Data Centric Audit project?

114. Have all involved Data Centric Audit project stakeholders and work groups committed to the Data Centric Audit project?

115. The greatest degree of uncertainty is encountered during which phase of the Data Centric Audit project life cycle?

116. What do you need to do to accomplish the goal or goals?

117. Is there a scope management plan that includes how Data Centric Audit project scope will be defined, developed, monitored, validated and controlled?

118. Has a provision been made to reassess Data Centric Audit project risks at various Data Centric Audit project stages?

119. Has your organization readiness assessment been conducted?

120. Will your organizations estimating methodology be used and followed?

121. What are the risks that could significantly affect the scope of the Data Centric Audit project?

122. Do you have the reasons why the changes to your organizational systems and capabilities are required?

123. Is there a Data Centric Audit project organization chart showing the reporting relationships and responsibilities for each position?

124. Are tasks tracked by hours?

125. Has a proper Data Centric Audit project work location been established that will allow the team to work together with user personnel?

126. Are the results of quality assurance reviews provided to affected groups & individuals?

127. What are the risks that could significantly affect the budget of the Data Centric Audit project?

128. What strengths do you have?

2.3 Requirements Management Plan: Data Centric Audit

129. Do you understand the role that each stakeholder will play in the requirements process?

130. Did you use declarative statements?

131. How do you know that you have done this right?

132. Who is responsible for monitoring and tracking the Data Centric Audit project requirements?

133. How will the requirements become prioritized?

134. How will the information be distributed?

135. In case of software development; Should you have a test for each code module?

136. What is the earliest finish date for this Data Centric Audit project if it is scheduled to start on ...?

137. The wbs is developed as part of a joint planning session. and how do you know that you have done this right?

138. Who will do the reporting and to whom will reports be delivered?

139. What went wrong?

140. Will you perform a Requirements Risk assessment

and develop a plan to deal with risks?

141. Are actual resource expenditures versus planned still acceptable?

142. Will the contractors involved take full responsibility?

143. Do you really need to write this document at all?

144. After the requirements are gathered and set forth on the requirements register, theyre little more than a laundry list of items. Some may be duplicates, some might conflict with others and some will be too broad or too vague to understand. Describe how the requirements will be analyzed. Who will perform the analysis?

145. What cost metrics will be used?

146. If it exists, where is it housed?

147. What went right?

148. Who has the authority to reject Data Centric Audit project requirements?

2.4 Requirements Documentation: Data Centric Audit

149. Have the benefits identified with the system being identified clearly?

150. How to document system requirements?

151. Where do system and software requirements come from, what are sources?

152. How do you know when a Requirement is accurate enough?

153. Who provides requirements?

154. Verifiability. can the requirements be checked?

155. Who is involved?

156. Basic work/business process; high-level, what is being touched?

157. Is your business case still valid?

158. Can the requirements be checked?

159. Is new technology needed?

160. Can the requirement be changed without a large impact on other requirements?

161. Does the system provide the functions which

best support the customers needs?

162. Are all functions required by the customer included?

163. Is the requirement properly understood?

164. Who is interacting with the system?

165. What images does it conjure?

166. How does the proposed Data Centric Audit project contribute to the overall objectives of your organization?

167. If applicable; are there issues linked with the fact that this is an offshore Data Centric Audit project?

168. How much testing do you need to do to prove that your system is safe?

2.5 Requirements Traceability Matrix: Data Centric Audit

169. Do you have a clear understanding of all subcontracts in place?

170. How will it affect the stakeholders personally in career?

171. Why use a WBS?

172. Describe the process for approving requirements so they can be added to the traceability matrix and Data Centric Audit project work can be performed. Will the Data Centric Audit project requirements become approved in writing?

173. What percentage of Data Centric Audit projects are producing traceability matrices between requirements and other work products?

174. Is there a requirements traceability process in place?

175. Will you use a Requirements Traceability Matrix?

176. Why do you manage scope?

177. What are the chronologies, contingencies, consequences, criteria?

178. How small is small enough?

179. What is the WBS?

180. How do you manage scope?

2.6 Project Scope Statement: Data Centric Audit

181. Are there adequate Data Centric Audit project control systems?

182. Will tasks be marked complete only after QA has been successfully completed?

183. Change management vs. change leadership - what is the difference?

184. Is there a baseline plan against which to measure progress?

185. Has the format for tracking and monitoring schedules and costs been defined?

186. Will this process be communicated to the customer and Data Centric Audit project team?

187. Data Centric Audit project lead, team lead, solution architect?

188. Is there a Change Management Board?

189. Elements of scope management that deal with concept development ?

190. Is the Data Centric Audit project manager qualified and experienced in Data Centric Audit project management?

191. Has everyone approved the Data Centric Audit projects scope statement?

192. How will you verify the accuracy of the work of the Data Centric Audit project, and what constitutes acceptance of the deliverables?

193. What are the possible consequences should a risk come to occur?

194. Have the configuration management functions been assigned?

195. Is the Data Centric Audit project sponsor function identified and defined?

196. Will all Data Centric Audit project issues be unconditionally tracked through the issue resolution process?

197. What process would you recommend for creating the Data Centric Audit project scope statement?

198. Will you need a statement of work?

199. What is a process you might recommend to verify the accuracy of the research deliverable?

200. Is the quality function identified and assigned?

2.7 Assumption and Constraint Log: Data Centric Audit

201. Are formal code reviews conducted?

202. Does the document/deliverable meet general requirements (for example, statement of work) for all deliverables?

203. Does a specific action and/or state that is known to violate security policy occur?

204. What do you log?

205. If appropriate, is the deliverable content consistent with current Data Centric Audit project documents and in compliance with the Document Management Plan?

206. Are there standards for code development?

207. Has the approach and development strategy of the Data Centric Audit project been defined, documented and accepted by the appropriate stakeholders?

208. How many Data Centric Audit project staff does this specific process affect?

209. What weaknesses do you have?

210. Does a documented Data Centric Audit project organizational policy & plan (i.e. governance model)

exist?

211. Are there cosmetic errors that hinder readability and comprehension?

212. How relevant is this attribute to this Data Centric Audit project or audit?

213. How do you design an auditing system?

214. Was the document/deliverable developed per the appropriate or required standards (for example, Institute of Electrical and Electronics Engineers standards)?

215. Have Data Centric Audit project management standards and procedures been established and documented?

216. If it is out of compliance, should the process be amended or should the Plan be amended?

217. Were the system requirements formally reviewed prior to initiating the design phase?

218. How are new requirements or changes to requirements identified?

219. What do you audit?

2.8 Work Breakdown Structure: Data Centric Audit

220. What has to be done?

221. How far down?

222. Do you need another level?

223. How big is a work-package?

224. When do you stop?

225. What is the probability of completing the Data Centric Audit project in less that xx days?

226. How will you and your Data Centric Audit project team define the Data Centric Audit projects scope and work breakdown structure?

227. Is it still viable?

228. Is the work breakdown structure (wbs) defined and is the scope of the Data Centric Audit project clear with assigned deliverable owners?

229. How much detail?

230. Why would you develop a Work Breakdown Structure?

231. Who has to do it?

232. Is it a change in scope?

233. When does it have to be done?

234. Where does it take place?

235. How many levels?

2.9 WBS Dictionary: Data Centric Audit

236. Is data disseminated to the contractors management timely, accurate, and usable?

237. Are the bases and rates for allocating costs from each indirect pool consistently applied?

238. Are work packages reasonably short in time duration or do they have adequate objective indicators/milestones to minimize subjectivity of the in process work evaluation?

239. Are estimates developed by Data Centric Audit project personnel coordinated with the already stated responsible for overall management to determine whether required resources will be available according to revised planning?

240. Are overhead budgets and costs being handled according to the disclosure statement when applicable, or otherwise properly classified (for example, engineering overhead, IR&D)?

241. Is work properly classified as measured effort, LOE, or apportioned effort and appropriately separated?

242. Are time-phased budgets established for planning and control of level of effort activity by category of resource; for example, type of manpower and/or material?

243. Are overhead cost budgets (or Data Centric Audit projections) established on a facility-wide basis at least annually for the life of the contract?

244. Are the latest revised estimates of costs at completion compared with the established budgets at appropriate levels and causes of variances identified?

245. Does the contractors system provide unit or lot costs when applicable?

246. Are all authorized tasks assigned to identified organizational elements?

247. Does the accounting system provide a basis for auditing records of direct costs chargeable to the contract?

248. Does the cost accumulation system provide for summarization of indirect costs from the point of allocation to the contract total?

249. Is the anticipated (firm and potential) business base Data Centric Audit projected in a rational, consistent manner?

250. Appropriate work authorization documents which subdivide the contractual effort and responsibilities, within functional organizations?

251. Does the scheduling system identify in a timely manner the status of work?

252. Are data being used by managers in an effective

manner to ascertain Data Centric Audit project or functional status, to identify reasons or significant variance, and to initiate appropriate corrective action?

2.10 Schedule Management Plan: Data Centric Audit

253. Quality assurance overheads?

254. Is there a formal set of procedures supporting Issues Management?

255. Do Data Centric Audit project managers participating in the Data Centric Audit project know the Data Centric Audit projects true status first hand?

256. Are any non-compliance issues that exist due to your organizations practices communicated to your organization?

257. Does the time Data Centric Audit projection include an amount for contingencies (time reserves)?

258. Will rolling way planning be used?

259. Is stakeholder involvement adequate?

260. Has the ims been resource-loaded and are assigned resources reasonable and available?

261. How relevant is this attribute to this Data Centric Audit project or audit?

262. Are all resource assumptions documented?

263. Are Data Centric Audit project team members committed fulltime?

264. Is there a procedure for management, control and release of schedule margin?

265. Are all activities captured and do they address all approved work scope in the Data Centric Audit project baseline?

266. Are decisions captured in a decisions log?

267. Time for overtime?

268. Does the ims include all contract and/or designated management control milestones?

269. Were stakeholders aware and supportive of the principles and practices of modern software estimation?

270. Why time management?

271. Alignment to strategic goals & objectives?

2.11 Activity List: Data Centric Audit

272. What went well?

273. How will it be performed?

274. Can you determine the activity that must finish, before this activity can start?

275. How difficult will it be to do specific activities on this Data Centric Audit project?

276. What is the probability the Data Centric Audit project can be completed in xx weeks?

277. What did not go as well?

278. How much slack is available in the Data Centric Audit project?

279. What is your organizations history in doing similar activities?

280. Are the required resources available or need to be acquired?

281. What are you counting on?

282. Is there anything planned that does not need to be here?

283. In what sequence?

284. What will be performed?

285. What is the LF and LS for each activity?

286. How do you determine the late start (LS) for each activity?

287. Is infrastructure setup part of your Data Centric Audit project?

288. Where will it be performed?

289. What are the critical bottleneck activities?

2.12 Activity Attributes: Data Centric Audit

290. How many days do you need to complete the work scope with a limit of X number of resources?

291. Activity: what is Missing?

292. Which method produces the more accurate cost assignment?

293. Would you consider either of corresponding activities an outlier?

294. Have you identified the Activity Leveling Priority code value on each activity?

295. What conclusions/generalizations can you draw from this?

296. Does your organization of the data change its meaning?

297. How do you manage time?

298. Were there other ways you could have organized the data to achieve similar results?

299. How else could the items be grouped?

300. How difficult will it be to do specific activities on this Data Centric Audit project?

301. How many resources do you need to complete the work scope within a limit of X number of days?

302. Resource is assigned to?

303. Activity: fair or not fair?

304. Where else does it apply?

305. Is there a trend during the year?

306. Can you re-assign any activities to another resource to resolve an over-allocation?

2.13 Milestone List: Data Centric Audit

307. Identify critical paths (one or more) and which activities are on the critical path?

308. How will you get the word out to customers?

309. Obstacles faced?

310. What has been done so far?

311. Vital contracts and partners?

312. Insurmountable weaknesses?

313. Which path is the critical path?

314. When will the Data Centric Audit project be complete?

315. Can you derive how soon can the whole Data Centric Audit project finish?

316. Reliability of data, plan predictability?

317. What is the market for your technology, product or service?

318. Competitive advantages?

319. Sustainable financial backing?

320. How late can the activity finish?

321. What are your competitors vulnerabilities?

322. What background experience, skills, and strengths does the team bring to your organization?

323. How late can each activity be finished and started?

324. What specific improvements did you make to the Data Centric Audit project proposal since the previous time?

325. It is to be a narrative text providing the crucial aspects of your Data Centric Audit project proposal answering what, who, how, when and where?

2.14 Network Diagram: Data Centric Audit

326. How confident can you be in your milestone dates and the delivery date?

327. What job or jobs could run concurrently?

328. What job or jobs precede it?

329. If a current contract exists, can you provide the vendor name, contract start, and contract expiration date?

330. Are the required resources available?

331. Review the logical flow of the network diagram. Take a look at which activities you have first and then sequence the activities. Do they make sense?

332. What must be completed before an activity can be started?

333. Which type of network diagram allows you to depict four types of dependencies?

334. What are the Major Administrative Issues?

335. What are the Key Success Factors?

336. Will crashing x weeks return more in benefits than it costs?

337. Planning: who, how long, what to do?

338. Where do you schedule uncertainty time?

339. What to do and When?

340. What activity must be completed immediately before this activity can start?

341. What are the tools?

342. Can you calculate the confidence level?

343. What controls the start and finish of a job?

344. Exercise: what is the probability that the Data Centric Audit project duration will exceed xx weeks?

2.15 Activity Resource Requirements: Data Centric Audit

345. How do you handle petty cash?

346. When does monitoring begin?

347. Anything else?

348. Which logical relationship does the PDM use most often?

349. Do you use tools like decomposition and rolling-wave planning to produce the activity list and other outputs?

350. How many signatures do you require on a check and does this match what is in your policy and procedures?

351. Organizational Applicability?

352. Are there unresolved issues that need to be addressed?

353. Why do you do that?

354. What is the Work Plan Standard?

355. Other support in specific areas?

356. What are constraints that you might find during the Human Resource Planning process?

2.16 Resource Breakdown Structure: Data Centric Audit

357. Is predictive resource analysis being done?

358. What is the difference between % Complete and % work?

359. Why do you do it?

360. Who will use the system?

361. Which resource planning tool provides information on resource responsibility and accountability?

362. How difficult will it be to do specific activities on this Data Centric Audit project?

363. Who is allowed to see what data about which resources?

364. Why is this important?

365. Who is allowed to perform which functions?

366. What is each stakeholders desired outcome for the Data Centric Audit project?

367. Which resources should be in the resource pool?

368. What is the purpose of assigning and documenting responsibility?

369. What is the number one predictor of a groups productivity?

370. What defines a successful Data Centric Audit project?

371. Changes based on input from stakeholders?

372. What defines a successful Data Centric Audit project?

373. How can this help you with team building?

2.17 Activity Duration Estimates: Data Centric Audit

374. Why is it difficult to use Data Centric Audit project management software well?

375. Are activity dependencies documented?

376. Research risk management software. Are many products available?

377. What is the difference between using brainstorming and the Delphi technique for risk identification?

378. What are the Data Centric Audit project management deliverables of each process group?

379. Sigma Data Centric Audit project?

380. Does a process exist to formally recognize new Data Centric Audit projects?

381. Calculate the expected duration for an activity that has a most likely time of 3, a pessimistic time of 10, and a optimiztic time of 2?

382. How do you enter durations, link tasks, and view critical path information?

383. Consider the common sources of risk on information technology Data Centric Audit projects and suggestions for managing them. Which

suggestions do you find most useful?

384. Consider the changes in the job market for information technology workers. How does the job market and current state of the economy affect human resource management?

385. Where do schedules come from?

386. Who will promote it?

387. When would a milestone chart be used instead of a bar char?

388. How many different communications channels does a Data Centric Audit project team with six people have?

389. What is earned value?

390. Are procurement documents used to solicit accurate and complete proposals from prospective sellers?

391. How can others help Data Centric Audit project managers understand your organizational context for Data Centric Audit projects?

392. Which type of mathematical analysis is being used?

393. Are Data Centric Audit project costs tracked in the general ledger?

2.18 Duration Estimating Worksheet: Data Centric Audit

394. What utility impacts are there?

395. What is your role?

396. What is an Average Data Centric Audit project?

397. What info is needed?

398. When, then?

399. Is a construction detail attached (to aid in explanation)?

400. Can the Data Centric Audit project be constructed as planned?

401. Is this operation cost effective?

402. Does the Data Centric Audit project provide innovative ways for stakeholders to overcome obstacles or deliver better outcomes?

403. What questions do you have?

404. What work will be included in the Data Centric Audit project?

405. Will the Data Centric Audit project collaborate with the local community and leverage resources?

406. Done before proceeding with this activity or what can be done concurrently?

407. When do the individual activities need to start and finish?

408. Why estimate costs?

409. What is next?

410. Why estimate time and cost?

411. For other activities, how much delay can be tolerated?

2.19 Project Schedule: Data Centric Audit

412. What is the purpose of a Data Centric Audit project schedule?

413. What does that mean?

414. Are there activities that came from a template or previous Data Centric Audit project that are not applicable on this phase of this Data Centric Audit project?

415. Are the original Data Centric Audit project schedule and budget realistic?

416. How can slack be negative?

417. If you can not fix it, how do you do it differently?

418. Is infrastructure setup part of your Data Centric Audit project?

419. How do you know that youhave done this right?

420. How much slack is available in the Data Centric Audit project?

421. Your best shot for providing estimations how complex/how much work does the activity require?

422. Should you have a test for each code module?

423. Should you include sub-activities?

424. Are procedures defined by which the Data Centric Audit project schedule may be changed?

425. Why is this particularly bad?

426. Are you working on the right risks?

427. Verify that the update is accurate. Are all remaining durations correct?

428. Is there a Schedule Management Plan that establishes the criteria and activities for developing, monitoring and controlling the Data Centric Audit project schedule?

429. What documents, if any, will the subcontractor provide (eg Data Centric Audit project schedule, quality plan etc)?

2.20 Cost Management Plan: Data Centric Audit

430. Are risk triggers captured?

431. Are action items captured and managed?

432. The definition of the Data Centric Audit project scope what needs to be accomplished?

433. Are enough systems & user personnel assigned to the Data Centric Audit project?

434. Sensitivity analysis?

435. Was the Data Centric Audit project schedule reviewed by all stakeholders and formally accepted?

436. Have activity relationships and interdependencies within tasks been adequately identified?

437. Are vendor invoices audited for accuracy before payment?

438. Were the budget estimates reasonable?

439. Have key stakeholders been identified?

440. Were Data Centric Audit project team members involved in detailed estimating and scheduling?

441. Contingency – how will cost contingency be

administered?

442. Are written status reports provided on a designated frequent basis?

443. What will be the split of responsibilities of progress measurement and controls among the owner, contractor, subcontractors, and vendors?

444. Do Data Centric Audit project teams & team members report on status / activities / progress?

445. Forecasts – how will the time and resources needed to complete the Data Centric Audit project be forecast?

446. Is the structure for tracking the Data Centric Audit project schedule well defined and assigned to a specific individual?

447. What is Data Centric Audit project cost management?

448. Have the reasons why the changes to your organizational systems and capabilities are required?

2.21 Activity Cost Estimates: Data Centric Audit

449. How do you manage cost?

450. How do you change activities?

451. Measurable - are the targets measurable?

452. Can you delete activities or make them inactive?

453. How do you fund change orders?

454. What areas were overlooked on this Data Centric Audit project?

455. What makes a good expected result statement?

456. Are cost subtotals needed?

457. How do you treat administrative costs in the activity inventory?

458. Certification of actual expenditures?

459. The impact and what actions were taken?

460. Padding is bad and contingencies are good. what is the difference?

461. Who determines when the contractor is paid?

462. How do you allocate indirect costs to activities?

463. How many activities should you have?

464. Vac -variance at completion, how much over/ under budget do you expect to be?

465. Who determines the quality and expertise of contractors?

466. How and when do you enter into Data Centric Audit project Procurement Management?

2.22 Cost Estimating Worksheet: Data Centric Audit

467. What costs are to be estimated?

468. What is the estimated labor cost today based upon this information?

469. Is it feasible to establish a control group arrangement?

470. Can a trend be established from historical performance data on the selected measure and are the criteria for using trend analysis or forecasting methods met?

471. Identify the timeframe necessary to monitor progress and collect data to determine how the selected measure has changed?

472. Ask: are others positioned to know, are others credible, and will others cooperate?

473. What will others want?

474. What is the purpose of estimating?

475. Is the Data Centric Audit project responsive to community need?

476. How will the results be shared and to whom?

477. Does the Data Centric Audit project provide

innovative ways for stakeholders to overcome obstacles or deliver better outcomes?

478. What can be included?

479. What additional Data Centric Audit project(s) could be initiated as a result of this Data Centric Audit project?

480. Will the Data Centric Audit project collaborate with the local community and leverage resources?

481. What happens to any remaining funds not used?

482. Who is best positioned to know and assist in identifying corresponding factors?

483. Value pocket identification & quantification what are value pockets?

2.23 Cost Baseline: Data Centric Audit

484. Definition of done can be traced back to the definitions of what are you providing to the customer in terms of deliverables?

485. What can go wrong?

486. Is the cr within Data Centric Audit project scope?

487. Have all approved changes to the schedule baseline been identified and impact on the Data Centric Audit project documented?

488. What threats might prevent you from getting there?

489. When should cost estimates be developed?

490. What deliverables come first?

491. Has the Data Centric Audit projected annual cost to operate and maintain the product(s) or service(s) been approved and funded?

492. How will cost estimates be used?

493. Is the requested change request a result of changes in other Data Centric Audit project(s)?

494. Is there anything you need from upper management in order to be successful?

495. At which frequency ?

496. How likely is it to go wrong?

497. Have the resources used by the Data Centric Audit project been reassigned to other units or Data Centric Audit projects?

498. How accurate do cost estimates need to be?

499. Have all approved changes to the cost baseline been identified and impact on the Data Centric Audit project documented?

500. On time?

501. Where do changes come from?

2.24 Quality Management Plan: Data Centric Audit

502. Who gets results of work?

503. How do you manage quality?

504. How are training records kept?

505. After observing execution of process, is it in compliance with the documented Plan?

506. Has a Data Centric Audit project Communications Plan been developed?

507. Have Data Centric Audit project management standards and procedures been established and documented?

508. Results Available?

509. What are you trying to accomplish?

510. How do you ensure that protocols are up to date?

511. Show/provide copy of procedures for taking field notes?

512. Checking the completeness and appropriateness of the sampling and testing. Were the right locations/samples tested for the right parameters?

513. What is the return on investment?

514. Is this process still needed?

515. How are calibration records kept?

516. Is there a Steering Committee in place?

517. What process do you use to minimize errors, defects, and rework?

518. How does your organization decide what to measure?

519. Are qmps good forever?

2.25 Quality Metrics: Data Centric Audit

520. Are applicable standards referenced and available?

521. How do you calculate corresponding metrics?

522. What metrics do you measure?

523. Where is quality now?

524. How effective are your security tests?

525. What is the benchmark?

526. If the defect rate during testing is substantially higher than that of the previous release (or a similar product), then ask: Did you plan for and actually improve testing effectiveness?

527. Are interface issues coordinated?

528. Were number of defects identified?

529. Were quality attributes reported?

530. Who is willing to lead?

531. Are there already quality metrics available that detect nonlinear embeddings and trends similar to the users perception?

532. There are many reasons to shore up quality-related metrics, and what metrics are important?

533. What forces exist that would cause them to change?

534. How do you measure?

535. What are your organizations expectations for its quality Data Centric Audit project?

536. Did evaluation start on time?

537. Was the overall quality better or worse than previous products?

538. What happens if you get an abnormal result?

539. What is the timeline to meet your goal?

2.26 Process Improvement Plan: Data Centric Audit

540. Are you making progress on the improvement framework?

541. What personnel are the change agents for your initiative?

542. Does explicit definition of the measures exist?

543. Are you meeting the quality standards?

544. Does your process ensure quality?

545. Management commitment at all levels?

546. Where do you want to be?

547. What lessons have you learned so far?

548. To elicit goal statements, do you ask a question such as, What do you want to achieve?

549. Are you following the quality standards?

550. Who should prepare the process improvement action plan?

551. What is quality and how will you ensure it?

552. Why quality management?

553. Has a process guide to collect the data been developed?

554. Are you making progress on the goals?

555. What personnel are the coaches for your initiative?

556. Has the time line required to move measurement results from the points of collection to databases or users been established?

557. Everyone agrees on what process improvement is, right?

2.27 Responsibility Assignment Matrix: Data Centric Audit

558. Are management actions taken to reduce indirect costs when there are significant adverse variances?

559. What do you do when people do not respond?

560. What travel needed?

561. Too many is: do all the identified roles need to be routinely informed or only in exceptional circumstances?

562. Which Data Centric Audit project management knowledge area is least mature?

563. Are the wbs and organizational levels for application of the Data Centric Audit projected overhead costs identified?

564. Does the contractor use objective results, design reviews, and tests to trace schedule?

565. Do others have the time to dedicate to your Data Centric Audit project?

566. Does the contractor use objective results, design reviews and tests to trace schedule performance?

567. What are some important Data Centric Audit project communications management tools?

568. What materials and procurements needed?

569. Why cost benefit analysis?

570. Are all elements of indirect expense identified to overhead cost budgets of Data Centric Audit projections?

571. Do you know how your people are allocated?

572. Are people afraid to let you know when others are under allocated?

573. Incurrence of actual indirect costs in excess of budgets, by element of expense?

574. Are authorized changes being incorporated in a timely manner?

2.28 Roles and Responsibilities: Data Centric Audit

575. What is working well?

576. Are Data Centric Audit project team roles and responsibilities identified and documented?

577. Is the data complete?

578. Once the responsibilities are defined for the Data Centric Audit project, have the deliverables, roles and responsibilities been clearly communicated to every participant?

579. Concern: where are you limited or have no authority, where you can not influence?

580. Is feedback clearly communicated and non-judgmental?

581. Are the quality assurance functions and related roles and responsibilities clearly defined?

582. What should you highlight for improvement?

583. Is there a training program in place for stakeholders covering expectations, roles and responsibilities and any addition knowledge others need to be good stakeholders?

584. Who: who is involved?

585. How well did the Data Centric Audit project Team understand the expectations of specific roles and responsibilities?

586. Accountabilities: what are the roles and responsibilities of individual team members?

587. Key conclusions and recommendations: Are conclusions and recommendations relevant and acceptable?

588. Attainable / achievable: the goal is attainable; can you actually accomplish the goal?

589. What specific behaviors did you observe?

590. Who is responsible for implementation activities and where will the functions, roles and responsibilities be defined?

591. Be specific; avoid generalities. Thank you and great work alone are insufficient. What exactly do you appreciate and why?

592. What should you do now to ensure that you are exceeding expectations and excelling in your current position?

593. Have you ever been a part of this team?

594. What should you do now to ensure that you are meeting all expectations of your current position?

2.29 Human Resource Management Plan: Data Centric Audit

595. Staffing Requirements?

596. Responsiveness to change and the resulting demands for different skills and abilities?

597. What is this Data Centric Audit project aiming to achieve?

598. Are software metrics formally captured, analyzed and used as a basis for other Data Centric Audit project estimates?

599. Are Data Centric Audit project team members committed fulltime?

600. How do you determine what key skills and talents are needed to meet the objectives. Is your organization primarily focused on a specific industry?

601. Are enough systems & user personnel assigned to the Data Centric Audit project?

602. Is the assigned Data Centric Audit project manager a PMP (Certified Data Centric Audit project manager) and experienced?

603. Who is evaluated?

604. Where is your organization headed?

605. What areas does the group agree are the biggest success on the Data Centric Audit project?

606. Are the Data Centric Audit project plans updated on a frequent basis?

607. Are status reports received per the Data Centric Audit project Plan?

608. Are corrective actions and variances reported?

609. Has a provision been made to reassess Data Centric Audit project risks at various Data Centric Audit project stages?

610. What were things that you did very well and want to do the same again on the next Data Centric Audit project?

2.30 Communications Management Plan: Data Centric Audit

611. Can you think of other people who might have concerns or interests?

612. Are others needed?

613. How were corresponding initiatives successful?

614. Are there common objectives between the team and the stakeholder?

615. What approaches do you use?

616. Why do you manage communications?

617. What are the interrelationships?

618. Timing: when do the effects of the communication take place?

619. Do you feel more overwhelmed by stakeholders?

620. Who to learn from?

621. What to know?

622. Do you have members of your team responsible for certain stakeholders?

623. Will messages be directly related to the release strategy or phases of the Data Centric Audit project?

624. Who did you turn to if you had questions?

625. Do you prepare stakeholder engagement plans?

626. Do you then often overlook a key stakeholder or stakeholder group?

627. What approaches to you feel are the best ones to use?

628. How do you manage communications?

629. Is the stakeholder role recognized by your organization?

630. Are there potential barriers between the team and the stakeholder?

2.31 Risk Management Plan: Data Centric Audit

631. Which risks should get the attention?

632. What would you do differently?

633. How is the audit profession changing?

634. Do you have a consistent repeatable process that is actually used?

635. Is the customer willing to establish rapid communication links with the developer?

636. Market risk: will the new product be useful to your organization or marketable to others?

637. Are end-users enthusiastically committed to the Data Centric Audit project and the system/product to be built?

638. Is a software Data Centric Audit project management tool available?

639. How well were you able to manage your risk before?

640. Financial risk -can your organization afford to undertake the Data Centric Audit project?

641. What did not work so well?

642. Is there additional information that would make you more confident about your analysis?

643. Have customers been involved fully in the definition of requirements?

644. Do requirements put excessive performance constraints on the product?

645. How can you fix it?

646. Are the participants able to keep up with the workload?

647. Minimize cost and financial risk?

648. Can the Data Centric Audit project proceed without assuming the risk?

2.32 Risk Register: Data Centric Audit

649. Assume the risk event or situation happens, what would the impact be?

650. Contingency actions - planned actions to reduce the immediate seriousness of the risk when it does occur. What should you do when?

651. What will be done?

652. What further options might be available for responding to the risk?

653. What is the reason for current performance gaps and do the risks and opportunities identified previously account for this?

654. What risks might negatively or positively affect achieving the Data Centric Audit project objectives?

655. Does the evidence highlight any areas to advance opportunities or foster good relations. If yes what steps will be taken?

656. Methodology: how will risk management be performed on this Data Centric Audit project?

657. What is your current and future risk profile?

658. Preventative actions - planned actions to reduce the likelihood a risk will occur and/or reduce the seriousness should it occur. What should you do now?

659. Who needs to know about this?

660. Who is accountable?

661. What action, if any, has been taken to respond to the risk?

662. Are there any knock-on effects/impact on any of the other areas?

663. Having taken action, how did the responses effect change, and where is the Data Centric Audit project now?

664. Is further information required before making a decision?

665. Schedule impact/severity estimated range (workdays) assume the event happens, what is the potential impact?

666. Technology risk -is the Data Centric Audit project technically feasible?

667. What are you going to do to limit the Data Centric Audit projects risk exposure due to the identified risks?

2.33 Probability and Impact Assessment: Data Centric Audit

668. How do risks change during a Data Centric Audit project life cycle?

669. Why has this particular mode of contracting been chosen?

670. Workarounds are determined during which step of risk management?

671. Are the risk data timely and relevant?

672. How is risk handled within this Data Centric Audit project organization?

673. Do you have specific methods that you use for each phase of the process?

674. What will be the likely political environment during the life of the Data Centric Audit project?

675. What is the probability of the risk occurring?

676. How will economic events and trends likely affect the Data Centric Audit project?

677. What will be the likely political situation during the life of the Data Centric Audit project?

678. What are the industrial relations prevailing in your organization?

679. Is the customer willing to commit significant time to the requirements gathering process?

680. What will be cost of redeployment of personnel?

681. Can the risk be avoided by choosing a different alternative?

682. How do risks change during the Data Centric Audit projects life cycle?

683. Who should be responsible for the monitoring and tracking of the indicators youhave identified?

684. What is the risk appetite?

685. What risks does your organization have if the Data Centric Audit projects fail to meet deadline?

686. Are tool mentors available?

687. Do the requirements require the creation of new algorithms?

2.34 Probability and Impact Matrix: Data Centric Audit

688. Do the people have the right combinations of skills?

689. What do you expect?

690. Have you worked with the customer in the past?

691. During which risk management process is a determination to transfer a risk made?

692. What is your anticipated volatility of the requirements?

693. Can it be enlarged by drawing people from other areas of your organization?

694. How risk averse are you?

695. What is the level of experience available with your organization?

696. Can you handle the investment risk?

697. What should be done NEXT?

698. Are testing tools available and suitable?

699. Are you on schedule?

700. How are the local factors going to affect the

absorption?

701. During Data Centric Audit project executing, a team member identifies a risk that is not in the risk register. What should you do?

702. Can the Data Centric Audit project proceed without assuming the risk?

703. How are you working with risks?

704. Is the present organizational structure for handling the Data Centric Audit project sufficient?

705. What is the likely future demand of the customer?

706. How well were you able to manage your risk?

707. Amount of reused software?

2.35 Risk Data Sheet: Data Centric Audit

708. Type of risk identified?

709. Whom do you serve (customers)?

710. What will be the consequences if the risk happens?

711. During work activities could hazards exist?

712. How can it happen?

713. What is the likelihood of it happening?

714. Has the most cost-effective solution been chosen?

715. What if client refuses?

716. Who has a vested interest in how you perform as your organization (our stakeholders)?

717. What are the main opportunities available to you that you should grab while you can?

718. Risk of what?

719. What can happen?

720. What were the Causes that contributed?

721. How do you handle product safely?

722. Has a sensitivity analysis been carried out?

723. What are you trying to achieve (Objectives)?

724. What are your core values?

725. Are new hazards created?

726. What are you here for (Mission)?

727. What can you do?

2.36 Procurement Management Plan: Data Centric Audit

728. Has the Data Centric Audit project manager been identified?

729. Have all documents been archived in a Data Centric Audit project repository for each release?

730. Is there a requirements change management processes in place?

731. If independent estimates will be needed as evaluation criteria, who will prepare them and when?

732. Is there a set of procedures defining the scope, procedures, and deliverables defining quality control?

733. Similar Data Centric Audit projects?

734. Are all payments made according to the contract(s)?

735. Have reserves been created to address risks?

736. Are Data Centric Audit project team roles and responsibilities identified and documented?

737. Is a pmo (Data Centric Audit project management office) in place which provides oversight to the Data Centric Audit project?

738. Are meeting objectives identified for each

meeting?

739. Are trade-offs between accepting the risk and mitigating the risk identified?

740. What types of contracts will be used?

741. Has the Data Centric Audit project scope been baselined?

742. What areas are overlooked on this Data Centric Audit project?

743. Is there general agreement & acceptance of the current status and progress of the Data Centric Audit project?

744. Is there a formal set of procedures supporting Stakeholder Management?

745. Has the business need been clearly defined?

2.37 Source Selection Criteria: Data Centric Audit

746. Have team members been adequately trained?

747. How long will it take for the purchase cost to be the same as the lease cost?

748. Do you want to have them collaborate at subfactor level?

749. Who is entitled to a debriefing?

750. What information may not be provided?

751. Who should attend debriefings?

752. Are types/quantities of material, facilities appropriate?

753. Are there any specific considerations that precludes offers from being selected as the awardee?

754. What should communications be used to accomplish?

755. What evidence should be provided regarding proposal evaluations?

756. Do you have designated specific forms or worksheets?

757. What source selection software is your team

using?

758. Can you prevent comparison of proposals?

759. How much past performance information should be requested?

760. Can you make a cost/technical tradeoff?

761. Can you reasonably estimate total organization requirements for the coming year?

762. Is experience evaluated?

763. Are considerations anticipated?

764. What are the most common types of rating systems?

765. What are the most critical evaluation criteria that prove to be tiebreakers in the evaluation of proposals?

2.38 Stakeholder Management Plan: Data Centric Audit

766. Have Data Centric Audit project management standards and procedures been established and documented?

767. Has a resource management plan been created?

768. In your opinion, do certain Data Centric Audit project resources hold a higher importance than other resources?

769. Are there processes in place to ensure internal consistency between the source code components?

770. Has a quality assurance plan been developed for the Data Centric Audit project?

771. Have all stakeholders been identified?

772. Is it standard practice to formally commit stakeholders to the Data Centric Audit project via agreements?

773. How will the equipment be verified?

774. Are parking lot items captured?

775. What action will be taken once reports have been received?

776. Are Data Centric Audit project leaders committed

to this Data Centric Audit project full time?

777. Who might be involved in developing a charter?

778. Is the Data Centric Audit project sponsor clearly communicating the business case or rationale for why this Data Centric Audit project is needed?

779. Is an industry recognized mechanized support tool(s) being used for Data Centric Audit project scheduling & tracking?

780. Have stakeholder accountabilities & responsibilities been clearly defined?

781. How are the overall Data Centric Audit project development processes to be undertaken to produce the Data Centric Audit project outputs?

782. Are vendor contract reports, reviews and visits conducted periodically?

783. Does the plan conform to standards?

2.39 Change Management Plan: Data Centric Audit

784. Clearly articulate the overall business benefits of the Data Centric Audit project -why are you doing this now?

785. When developing your communication plan do you address : When should the given message be communicated?

786. Is there a need for new relationships to be built?

787. What provokes organizational change?

788. Different application of an existing process?

789. Who will fund the training?

790. What does a resilient organization look like?

791. What work practices will be affected?

792. Who might be able to help you the most?

793. What did the people around you say about it?

794. Is there support for this application(s) and are the details available for distribution?

795. Why would a Data Centric Audit project run more smoothly when change management is emphasized from the beginning?

796. What are the specific target groups/audiences that will be impacted by this change?

797. How does the principle of senders and receivers make the Data Centric Audit project communications effort more complex?

798. Do you need new systems?

799. How badly can information be misinterpreted?

800. What risks may occur upfront?

801. What policies and procedures need to be changed?

3.0 Executing Process Group: Data Centric Audit

802. Is the Data Centric Audit project making progress in helping to achieve the set results?

803. Have operating capacities been created and/or reinforced in partners?

804. How is Data Centric Audit project performance information created and distributed?

805. How do you measure difficulty?

806. Does software appear easy to learn?

807. What does it mean to take a systems view of a Data Centric Audit project?

808. What are the critical steps involved with strategy mapping?

809. Why should Data Centric Audit project managers strive to make jobs look easy?

810. What are deliverables of your Data Centric Audit project?

811. When is the appropriate time to bring the scorecard to Board meetings?

812. What will you do to minimize the impact should a risk event occur?

813. Do Data Centric Audit project managers understand your organizational context for Data Centric Audit projects?

814. Based on your Data Centric Audit project communication management plan, what worked well?

815. Were sponsors and decision makers available when needed outside regularly scheduled meetings?

816. What were things that you did well, and could improve, and how?

817. What are the challenges Data Centric Audit project teams face?

818. How can software assist in procuring goods and services?

819. What type of information goes in the quality assurance plan?

820. How does the job market and current state of the economy affect human resource management?

821. Are the necessary foundations in place to ensure the sustainability of the results of the programme?

3.1 Team Member Status Report: Data Centric Audit

822. Are the attitudes of staff regarding Data Centric Audit project work improving?

823. How much risk is involved?

824. What specific interest groups do you have in place?

825. How can you make it practical?

826. How will resource planning be done?

827. Do you have an Enterprise Data Centric Audit project Management Office (EPMO)?

828. How does this product, good, or service meet the needs of the Data Centric Audit project and your organization as a whole?

829. Does every department have to have a Data Centric Audit project Manager on staff?

830. Does the product, good, or service already exist within your organization?

831. How it is to be done?

832. Are the products of your organizations Data Centric Audit projects meeting customers objectives?

833. What is to be done?

834. Are your organizations Data Centric Audit projects more successful over time?

835. Why is it to be done?

836. Is there evidence that staff is taking a more professional approach toward management of your organizations Data Centric Audit projects?

837. The problem with Reward & Recognition Programs is that the truly deserving people all too often get left out. How can you make it practical?

838. When a teams productivity and success depend on collaboration and the efficient flow of information, what generally fails them?

839. Does your organization have the means (staff, money, contract, etc.) to produce or to acquire the product, good, or service?

840. Will the staff do training or is that done by a third party?

3.2 Change Request: Data Centric Audit

841. What are the duties of the change control team?

842. How does your organization control changes before and after software is released to a customer?

843. What must be taken into consideration when introducing change control programs?

844. When do you create a change request?

845. How many times must the change be modified or presented to the change control board before it is approved?

846. Why do you want to have a change control system?

847. What is the change request log?

848. Are there requirements attributes that are strongly related to the occurrence of defects and failures?

849. Will the change use memory to the extent that other functions will be not have sufficient memory to operate effectively?

850. What needs to be communicated?

851. Who can suggest changes?

852. Who will perform the change?

853. Will there be a change request form in use?

854. Have all related configuration items been properly updated?

855. Screen shots or attachments included in a Change Request?

856. How fast will change requests be approved?

857. Is it feasible to use requirements attributes as predictors of reliability?

858. How can changes be graded?

3.3 Change Log: Data Centric Audit

859. Should a more thorough impact analysis be conducted?

860. Does the suggested change request seem to represent a necessary enhancement to the product?

861. Do the described changes impact on the integrity or security of the system?

862. How does this change affect the timeline of the schedule?

863. Is the change request within Data Centric Audit project scope?

864. How does this change affect scope?

865. Is the change backward compatible without limitations?

866. Does the suggested change request represent a desired enhancement to the products functionality?

867. Will the Data Centric Audit project fail if the change request is not executed?

868. Is the submitted change a new change or a modification of a previously approved change?

869. How does this relate to the standards developed for specific business processes?

870. Is this a mandatory replacement?

871. Is the change request open, closed or pending?

872. When was the request submitted?

873. Who initiated the change request?

874. When was the request approved?

875. Is the requested change request a result of changes in other Data Centric Audit project(s)?

3.4 Decision Log: Data Centric Audit

876. How does the use a Decision Support System influence the strategies/tactics or costs?

877. How do you define success?

878. How consolidated and comprehensive a story can you tell by capturing currently available incident data in a central location and through a log of key decisions during an incident?

879. Adversarial environment. is your opponent open to a non-traditional workflow, or will it likely challenge anything you do?

880. Linked to original objective?

881. Which variables make a critical difference?

882. What is your overall strategy for quality control / quality assurance procedures?

883. Does anything need to be adjusted?

884. Who is the decisionmaker?

885. What alternatives/risks were considered?

886. What eDiscovery problem or issue did your organization set out to fix or make better?

887. What makes you different or better than others companies selling the same thing?

888. What is the line where eDiscovery ends and document review begins?

889. Is your opponent open to a non-traditional workflow, or will it likely challenge anything you do?

890. Decision-making process; how will the team make decisions?

891. It becomes critical to track and periodically revisit both operational effectiveness; Are you noticing all that you need to, and are you interpreting what you see effectively?

892. Meeting purpose; why does this team meet?

893. Do strategies and tactics aimed at less than full control reduce the costs of management or simply shift the cost burden?

894. How does an increasing emphasis on cost containment influence the strategies and tactics used?

895. What was the rationale for the decision?

3.5 Quality Audit: Data Centric Audit

896. Does the suppliers quality system have a written procedure for corrective action when a defect occurs?

897. Are goals well supported with strategies, operational plans, manuals and training?

898. How does your organization know that its policy management system is appropriately effective and constructive?

899. Are all employees including salespersons made aware that they must report all complaints received from any source for inclusion in the complaint handling system?

900. Have personnel cleanliness and health requirements been established?

901. Are training programs documented?

902. Are all records associated with the reconditioning of a device maintained for a minimum of two years after the sale or disposal of the last device within a lot of merchandise?

903. How does your organization know that its public relations and marketing systems are appropriately effective and constructive?

904. What does an analysis of your organizations staff profile suggest in terms of its planning, and how is this being addressed?

905. Statements of intent remain exactly that until they are put into effect. The next step is to deploy the already stated intentions. In other words, do the plans happen in reality?

906. Is there a written corporate quality policy?

907. How does your organization know that its systems for assisting staff with career planning and employment placements are appropriately effective and constructive?

908. Is the reports overall tone appropriate?

909. For each device to be reconditioned, are device specifications, such as appropriate engineering drawings, component specifications and software specifications, maintained?

910. Are the review comments incorporated?

911. How does your organization know that the research supervision provided to its staff is appropriately effective and constructive?

912. How does your organization know whether they are adhering to mission and achieving objectives?

913. What happens if your organization fails its Quality Audit?

914. How does your organization know that the support for its staff is appropriately effective and constructive?

915. How does your organization know that the range and quality of its accommodation, catering and transportation services are appropriately effective and constructive?

3.6 Team Directory: Data Centric Audit

916. When does information need to be distributed?

917. Timing: when do the effects of communication take place?

918. Process decisions: do job conditions warrant additional actions to collect job information and document on-site activity?

919. Who will write the meeting minutes and distribute?

920. Process decisions: which organizational elements and which individuals will be assigned management functions?

921. Where should the information be distributed?

922. What are you going to deliver or accomplish?

923. How and in what format should information be presented?

924. Process decisions: is work progressing on schedule and per contract requirements?

925. Have you decided when to celebrate the Data Centric Audit projects completion date?

926. Does a Data Centric Audit project team directory list all resources assigned to the Data Centric Audit project?

927. How will the team handle changes?

928. Is construction on schedule?

929. Who are the Team Members?

930. Who will talk to the customer?

931. Decisions: is the most suitable form of contract being used?

932. Process decisions: are contractors adequately prosecuting the work?

933. Days from the time the issue is identified?

3.7 Team Operating Agreement: Data Centric Audit

934. Do you send out the agenda and meeting materials in advance?

935. Must your team members rely on the expertise of other members to complete tasks?

936. Did you prepare participants for the next meeting?

937. Are there more than two national cultures represented by your team?

938. Do you brief absent members after they view meeting notes or listen to a recording?

939. Do you ensure that all participants know how to use the required technology?

940. What is teaming?

941. What is a Virtual Team?

942. Resource allocation: how will individual team members account for time and expenses, and how will this be allocated in the team budget?

943. Do you ask participants to close laptops and place mobile devices on silent on the table while the meeting is in progress?

944. Do you call or email participants to ensure understanding, follow-through and commitment to the meeting outcomes?

945. How will group handle unplanned absences?

946. Did you draft the meeting agenda?

947. Do team members reside in more than two countries?

948. Are there the right people on your team?

949. Conflict resolution: how will disputes and other conflicts be mediated or resolved?

950. What is culture?

951. Are leadership responsibilities shared among team members (versus a single leader)?

952. Did you determine the technology methods that best match the messages to be communicated?

953. Seconds for members to respond?

3.8 Team Performance Assessment: Data Centric Audit

954. When does the medium matter?

955. Where to from here?

956. Lack of method variance in self-reported affect and perceptions at work: Reality or artifact?

957. What makes opportunities more or less obvious?

958. How hard do you try to make a good selection?

959. What do you think is the most constructive thing that could be done now to resolve considerations and disputes about method variance?

960. If you are worried about method variance before you collect data, what sort of design elements might you include to reduce or eliminate the threat of method variance?

961. How hard did you try to make a good selection?

962. To what degree can team members meet frequently enough to accomplish the teams ends?

963. Do you promptly inform members about major developments that may affect them?

964. Do friends perform better than acquaintances?

965. Can team performance be reliably measured in simulator and live exercises using the same assessment tool?

966. How does Data Centric Audit project termination impact Data Centric Audit project team members?

967. To what degree can the team measure progress against specific goals?

968. How do you keep key people outside the group informed about its accomplishments?

969. To what degree does the teams purpose contain themes that are particularly meaningful and memorable?

970. To what degree are sub-teams possible or necessary?

971. To what degree will the team adopt a concrete, clearly understood, and agreed-upon approach that will result in achievement of the teams goals?

972. To what degree are the goals ambitious?

3.9 Team Member Performance Assessment: Data Centric Audit

973. What are the key duties or tasks of the Ratee?

974. How are evaluation results utilized?

975. What is the role of the Reviewer?

976. What variables that affect team members achievement are within your control?

977. What is a significant fact or event?

978. How is your organizations Strategic Management System tied to performance measurement?

979. How are training activities developed from a technical perspective?

980. What specific plans do you have for developing effective cross-platform assessments in a blended learning environment?

981. Who they are?

982. To what degree do team members articulate the teams work approach?

983. How often should assessments be conducted?

984. New skills/knowledge gained this year?

985. What are acceptable governance changes?

986. To what degree do the goals specify concrete team work products?

987. Should a ratee get a copy of all the raters documents about the employees performance?

988. What qualities does a successful Team leader possess?

989. Who receives a benchmark visit?

990. What tools are available to determine whether all contract functional and compliance areas of performance objectives, measures, and incentives have been met?

991. Goals met?

3.10 Issue Log: Data Centric Audit

992. Why not more evaluators?

993. Are there too many who have an interest in some aspect of your work?

994. Who reported the issue?

995. Who is involved as you identify stakeholders?

996. Who are the members of the governing body?

997. Is access to the Issue Log controlled?

998. Is the issue log kept in a safe place?

999. Who is the stakeholder?

1000. How do you reply to this question; you am new here and managing this major program. How do you suggest you build your network?

1001. What does the stakeholder need from the team?

1002. Who needs to know and how much?

1003. What is a change?

1004. Do you often overlook a key stakeholder or stakeholder group?

1005. Who do you turn to if you have questions?

1006. What is a Stakeholder?

1007. Who were proponents/opponents?

1008. What is the impact on the risks?

4.0 Monitoring and Controlling Process Group: Data Centric Audit

1009. How were collaborations developed, and how are they sustained?

1010. In what way has the program come up with innovative measures for problem-solving?

1011. What is the timeline?

1012. Who needs to be engaged upfront to ensure use of results?

1013. Change, where should you look for problems?

1014. Is there sufficient funding available for this?

1015. What input will you be required to provide the Data Centric Audit project team?

1016. When will the Data Centric Audit project be done?

1017. What were things that you need to improve?

1018. Use: how will they use the information?

1019. What resources (both financial and non-financial) are available/needed?

1020. Is there adequate validation on required fields?

1021. Are the services being delivered?

1022. Is the schedule for the set products being met?

1023. What are the goals of the program?

1024. What good practices or successful experiences or transferable examples have been identified?

1025. What were things that you did very well and want to do the same again on the next Data Centric Audit project?

4.1 Project Performance Report: Data Centric Audit

1026. To what degree will the approach capitalize on and enhance the skills of all team members in a manner that takes into consideration other demands on members of the team?

1027. To what degree does the funding match the requirement?

1028. To what degree is there a sense that only the team can succeed?

1029. What degree are the relative importance and priority of the goals clear to all team members?

1030. To what degree are the demands of the task compatible with and converge with the mission and functions of the formal organization?

1031. To what degree does the teams purpose constitute a broader, deeper aspiration than just accomplishing short-term goals?

1032. To what degree does the teams work approach provide opportunity for members to engage in results-based evaluation?

1033. To what degree can team members vigorously define the teams purpose in considerations with others who are not part of the functioning team?

1034. To what degree do team members understand one anothers roles and skills?

1035. To what degree are the tasks requirements reflected in the flow and storage of information?

1036. To what degree does the formal organization make use of individual resources and meet individual needs?

1037. To what degree does the task meet individual needs?

1038. To what degree does the information network provide individuals with the information they require?

1039. To what degree are the demands of the task compatible with and converge with the relationships of the informal organization?

1040. What is the degree to which rules govern information exchange between individuals within your organization?

1041. To what degree will new and supplemental skills be introduced as the need is recognized?

1042. To what degree can the cognitive capacity of individuals accommodate the flow of information?

4.2 Variance Analysis: Data Centric Audit

1043. What should management do?

1044. How have the setting and use of standards changed over time?

1045. How does your organization allocate the cost of shared expenses and services?

1046. How do you identify and isolate causes of favorable and unfavorable cost and schedule variances?

1047. Are records maintained to show how management reserves are used?

1048. What was the cause of the increase in costs?

1049. Is cost and schedule performance measurement done in a consistent, systematic manner?

1050. How are material, labor, and overhead standards set?

1051. How do you manage changes in the nature of the overhead requirements?

1052. Are detailed work packages planned as far in advance as practicable?

1053. What causes selling price variance?

1054. Are all budgets assigned to control accounts?

1055. Did a new competitor enter the market?

1056. Are there externalities from having some customers, even if they are unprofitable in the short run?

1057. Who are responsible for the establishment of budgets and assignment of resources for overhead performance?

1058. Are there changes in the direct base to which overhead costs are allocated?

4.3 Earned Value Status: Data Centric Audit

1059. Earned value can be used in almost any Data Centric Audit project situation and in almost any Data Centric Audit project environment. it may be used on large Data Centric Audit projects, medium sized Data Centric Audit projects, tiny Data Centric Audit projects (in cut-down form), complex and simple Data Centric Audit projects and in any market sector. some people, of course, know all about earned value, they have used it for years - but perhaps not as effectively as they could have?

1060. When is it going to finish?

1061. How much is it going to cost by the finish?

1062. Verification is a process of ensuring that the developed system satisfies the stakeholders agreements and specifications; Are you building the product right? What do you verify?

1063. How does this compare with other Data Centric Audit projects?

1064. Where is evidence-based earned value in your organization reported?

1065. Where are your problem areas?

1066. What is the unit of forecast value?

1067. Are you hitting your Data Centric Audit projects targets?

1068. If earned value management (EVM) is so good in determining the true status of a Data Centric Audit project and Data Centric Audit project its completion, why is it that hardly any one uses it in information systems related Data Centric Audit projects?

1069. Validation is a process of ensuring that the developed system will actually achieve the stakeholders desired outcomes; Are you building the right product? What do you validate?

4.4 Risk Audit: Data Centric Audit

1070. Are you willing to seek legal advice when required?

1071. Are you meeting your legal, regulatory and compliance requirements - if not, why not?

1072. If applicable; are compilers and code generators available and suitable for the product to be built?

1073. How effective are your risk controls?

1074. Does your organization have a process for meeting its ongoing taxation obligations?

1075. Strategic business risk audit methodologies; are corresponding an attempt to sell other services, and is management becoming the client of the audit rather than the shareholder?

1076. What are the commonly used work arounds in high risk areas?

1077. How do you govern assets?

1078. What are the costs associated with late delivery or a defective product?

1079. Does your auditor understand your business?

1080. Do staff understand the extent of duty of care?

1081. What events or circumstances could affect the

achievement of your objectives?

1082. Does your organization have an up-to-date constitution?

1083. Who is responsible for what?

1084. Does your organization have a register of insurance policies detailing all current insurance policies?

1085. Is the auditor able to evaluate contradictory evidence in an unbiased manner?

1086. Are staff committed for the duration of the product?

1087. Are all managers or operators of the facility or equipment competent or qualified?

1088. Do you meet all obligations relating to funds secured from grants, loans and sponsors?

4.5 Contractor Status Report: Data Centric Audit

1089. What was the budget or estimated cost for your organizations services?

1090. What was the final actual cost?

1091. How does the proposed individual meet each requirement?

1092. How long have you been using the services?

1093. If applicable; describe your standard schedule for new software version releases. Are new software version releases included in the standard maintenance plan?

1094. Who can list a Data Centric Audit project as organization experience, your organization or a previous employee of your organization?

1095. What process manages the contracts?

1096. What was the actual budget or estimated cost for your organizations services?

1097. Are there contractual transfer concerns?

1098. What was the overall budget or estimated cost?

1099. What are the minimum and optimal bandwidth requirements for the proposed solution?

1100. Describe how often regular updates are made to the proposed solution. Are corresponding regular updates included in the standard maintenance plan?

1101. How is risk transferred?

1102. What is the average response time for answering a support call?

4.6 Formal Acceptance: Data Centric Audit

1103. Was business value realized?

1104. Was the sponsor/customer satisfied?

1105. Who supplies data?

1106. What was done right?

1107. How well did the team follow the methodology?

1108. Was the Data Centric Audit project managed well?

1109. What is the Acceptance Management Process?

1110. Was the client satisfied with the Data Centric Audit project results?

1111. Was the Data Centric Audit project work done on time, within budget, and according to specification?

1112. What lessons were learned about your Data Centric Audit project management methodology?

1113. What are the requirements against which to test, Who will execute?

1114. Did the Data Centric Audit project achieve its MOV?

1115. Who would use it?

1116. Do you perform formal acceptance or burn-in tests?

1117. Have all comments been addressed?

1118. General estimate of the costs and times to complete the Data Centric Audit project?

1119. Does it do what Data Centric Audit project team said it would?

1120. How does your team plan to obtain formal acceptance on your Data Centric Audit project?

1121. Do you buy pre-configured systems or build your own configuration?

1122. What can you do better next time?

5.0 Closing Process Group: Data Centric Audit

1123. What were the desired outcomes?

1124. Were the outcomes different from the already stated planned?

1125. How well did the chosen processes fit the needs of the Data Centric Audit project?

1126. Is the Data Centric Audit project funded?

1127. What could be done to improve the process?

1128. Did the Data Centric Audit project team have enough people to execute the Data Centric Audit project plan?

1129. Did the delivered product meet the specified requirements and goals of the Data Centric Audit project?

1130. What level of risk does the proposed budget represent to the Data Centric Audit project?

1131. Who are the Data Centric Audit project stakeholders?

1132. Were decisions made in a timely manner?

1133. Just how important is your work to the overall success of the Data Centric Audit project?

1134. What areas does the group agree are the biggest success on the Data Centric Audit project?

1135. Based on your Data Centric Audit project communication management plan, what worked well?

1136. Are there funding or time constraints?

5.1 Procurement Audit: Data Centric Audit

1137. Did the conditions of contract comply with the detail provided in the procurement documents and with the outcome of the procurement procedure followed?

1138. What are the threats to supplier relations?

1139. Was the dynamic purchasing system set up following the rules of open procedure?

1140. Is a physical inventory taken periodically to verify fixed asset records?

1141. Are the right skills, experiences and competencies present in the acquisition workgroup and are the necessary outside specialists involved in part of the process?

1142. Did the contracting authority draw up a comprehensive written report about progress and outcome of the procurement process?

1143. Is it clear which procurement procedure your organization has opted for?

1144. Are procurement processes well organized and documented?

1145. Are open purchase orders with a fixed monetary limitation used for local purchases of small dollar value?

1146. Is there management monitoring of transactions and balances?

1147. Are travel expenditures monitored to determine that they are in line with other employees and reasonable for the area of travel?

1148. Did the contracting authority verify compliance with the basic requirements of the competition?

1149. Is the foreseen budget compared with similar Data Centric Audit projects or procurements yet realised (historical standards)?

1150. Were all admitted tenderers invited to submit a tender for each specific contract?

1151. Are proper financing arrangements taken?

1152. Was your organization specific about the nature and scope of the performance before launching the procurement process?

1153. Is electronic procurement applied to reduce transaction costs?

1154. Was the admissibility of variants displayed in the contract notice?

1155. Was the tender clearly and properly specified, including evaluation criteria and knowing about the market and therefore not over-prescriptive and receptive to innovation?

1156. Do the internal control systems function appropriate?

5.2 Contract Close-Out: Data Centric Audit

1157. Was the contract complete without requiring numerous changes and revisions?

1158. Are the signers the authorized officials?

1159. Was the contract sufficiently clear so as not to result in numerous disputes and misunderstandings?

1160. Parties: Authorized?

1161. Have all acceptance criteria been met prior to final payment to contractors?

1162. What happens to the recipient of services?

1163. How is the contracting office notified of the automatic contract close-out?

1164. Was the contract type appropriate?

1165. Have all contracts been closed?

1166. Parties: who is involved?

1167. How/when used ?

1168. Why Outsource?

1169. Have all contracts been completed?

1170. Change in attitude or behavior?

1171. Change in knowledge?

1172. How does it work?

1173. Has each contract been audited to verify acceptance and delivery?

1174. Change in circumstances?

1175. Have all contract records been included in the Data Centric Audit project archives?

1176. What is capture management?

5.3 Project or Phase Close-Out: Data Centric Audit

1177. In addition to assessing whether the Data Centric Audit project was successful, it is equally critical to analyze why it was or was not fully successful. Are you including this?

1178. What is a Risk?

1179. What information is each stakeholder group interested in?

1180. What are the informational communication needs for each stakeholder?

1181. Planned completion date?

1182. Did the delivered product meet the specified requirements and goals of the Data Centric Audit project?

1183. What can you do better next time, and what specific actions can you take to improve?

1184. Is there a clear cause and effect between the activity and the lesson learned?

1185. Was the schedule met?

1186. What benefits or impacts does the stakeholder group expect to obtain as a result of the Data Centric Audit project?

1187. What is this stakeholder expecting?

1188. Who is responsible for award close-out?

1189. Have business partners been involved extensively, and what data was required for them?

1190. Was the user/client satisfied with the end product?

1191. Did the Data Centric Audit project management methodology work?

1192. Who controlled key decisions that were made?

1193. What process was planned for managing issues/ risks?

1194. What are the marketing communication needs for each stakeholder?

5.4 Lessons Learned: Data Centric Audit

1195. What regulatory constraints impact the case?

1196. Are the lessons more complex and multivariate?

1197. How useful was your testing?

1198. Was the control overhead justified?

1199. How closely did deliverables match what was defined within the Data Centric Audit project Scope?

1200. How much communication is task-related?

1201. How effectively and timely was your organizational change impact identified and planned for?

1202. What is the expected lifespan of the deliverable?

1203. How does the budget cycle affect the case?

1204. What should have been accomplished during predeployment that was not accomplished?

1205. What is the proportion of in-house and contractor personnel authorized for the Data Centric Audit project?

1206. How well does the product or service the Data Centric Audit project produced meet your needs?

1207. Was the Data Centric Audit project manager sufficiently experienced, skilled, trained, supported?

1208. How smooth do you feel Integration has been?

1209. What are the funding priorities for intelligence?

1210. What would you change?

1211. What mistakes did you successfully avoid making?

1212. What are the skills directly related to the task?

1213. What are the expectations of the individuals?

Index

almost 243
already   123, 152, 184, 216, 225, 251
always 9
ambitious   232
amended   149
amount   19, 155, 203
amplify70, 106
analysis   2, 5, 9-10, 62, 66, 69-71, 84, 132, 136, 141, 166,
169, 174, 178, 189, 197, 205, 220, 224, 241
analyze   2, 58-59, 69, 258
analyzed   96, 128, 141, 192
annual 180
annually   153
another   150, 160
anothers   240
answer 10-11, 15, 27, 43, 58, 74, 89, 101
answered   25, 42, 57, 73, 88, 100, 125
answering   10, 162, 248
anybody   135
anyone   34, 104, 117
anything   157, 165, 180, 222-223
appear   1, 214
appetite   201
applicable   10, 143, 152-153, 172, 184, 245, 247
applied   91, 152, 254
appointed   38
appreciate   191
approach   50, 75, 77, 113, 121, 148, 217, 232-233, 239
approaches   79, 194-195
approval   35, 124
approve   128
approved   30, 65, 128, 136, 144, 147, 156, 180-181, 218-221
approving   144
architect   146
Architects   7
archived   206
archives   257
around114, 122, 212
arounds   245
articulate   212, 233
artifact231
ascertain   154
asking 1, 7

264

imbedded 97
immediate 198
impact 4, 40, 43, 47-49, 52-53, 79, 127, 142, 176, 180-181, 198-
200, 202, 214, 220, 232, 236, 260
impacted 45, 213
impacts 44, 54, 170, 258
implement 51, 68, 89
implicit 121
import 133
importance 210, 239
important 19, 24, 35, 59, 64, 66, 105, 114, 120-121, 123, 129,
134, 166, 185, 188, 251
improve 2, 9, 63, 74-75, 77, 79, 82, 84, 86-87, 184, 215, 237,
251, 258
improved 80, 83, 85, 90, 132
improving 76, 216
inactive 176
incentives 94, 234
incident 222
include 24, 75, 136, 155-156, 173, 231
included 2, 7, 55, 135, 143, 170, 179, 219, 247-248, 257
includes 9, 138
including 21, 29, 33, 37, 49, 54, 66, 94, 97, 224, 254, 258
inclusion 224
increase 109, 241
increased 113
increasing 111, 223
incurred 48
Incurrence 189
in-depth 8, 10
indicate 67, 96, 121
indicated 98
indicators 19, 49, 56, 59, 64, 68, 70, 78, 97, 152, 201
indirect 51, 152-153, 176, 188-189
indirectly 1
individual 1, 51, 171, 175, 191, 229, 240, 247
industrial 200
industry 92, 192, 211
infinite 103
influence 75, 102, 131, 190, 222-223
inform 231
informal 240
informed 115, 188, 232

material   152, 208, 241
materials   1, 189, 229
matrices   144
Matrix 2-4, 132, 144, 188, 202
matter 33, 49, 56, 231
mature 188
maximizing   104
meaning   159
meaningful   45, 111, 232
measurable   29, 40, 176
measure   2, 9, 20, 22, 31, 37, 43, 45-46, 49, 51-52, 54-55, 63,
66, 74, 78-79, 83, 86, 92, 95, 97-99, 146, 178, 183-185, 214, 232
measured   25, 46-48, 50-51, 53, 56-57, 85, 98, 100, 152, 232
measures   45, 49-52, 54-55, 59, 64, 66, 68, 78, 92, 96-97, 186,
234, 237
measuring   98
mechanical   1
mechanisms   134
mechanized   211
mediated   230
medium   231, 243
meeting   30, 96, 186, 191, 206-207, 216, 223, 227, 229-230,
245
meetings   27, 37-38, 214-215
megatrends   109
Member   5, 39, 119, 124, 203, 216, 233
members   36-37, 64, 95, 155, 174-175, 191-192, 194, 208,
228-233, 235, 239-240
memorable   232
memory   218
mentors   201
message   99, 212
messages   194, 230
method   134, 136, 159, 231
methods   32, 35, 52, 67, 138, 178, 200, 230
metrics 4, 39, 63, 94, 129, 141, 184-185, 192
milestone   3, 161, 163, 169
milestones   29, 131, 152, 156
minimize   127, 152, 183, 197, 214
minimizing   60, 104
minimum   224, 247
minority   19
minutes   30, 85, 227

process   1-7, 9, 27, 31, 35, 37-41, 55, 58-71, 83, 87, 90-94, 96, 98-99, 127, 134-135, 140, 142, 144, 146-149, 152, 165, 168, 182-183, 186-187, 196, 200-202, 212, 214, 223, 227-228, 237, 243-245, 247, 249, 251, 253-254, 259

processes   45, 48, 59-63, 65-68, 70-71, 94-95, 135, 206, 210-211, 220, 251, 253

procuring   215

produce   70, 129, 135, 165, 211, 217

produced   69, 84, 260

produces   159

producing   144

product   1, 56, 59, 64, 113, 129, 132, 161, 180, 184, 196-197, 205, 216-217, 220, 243-246, 251, 258-260

production   34, 83, 113

products   1, 17, 22, 112, 120, 129, 144, 168, 185, 216, 220, 234, 238

profession   196

profile 198, 224

program   24, 51, 72, 94, 135, 190, 235, 237-238

programme   215

programs   217-218, 224

progress   38, 46, 79, 112, 146, 175, 178, 186-187, 207, 214, 229, 232, 253

project 2-8, 18, 20, 25, 29, 52, 60, 71, 89-90, 97, 101, 104-106, 108, 114, 117, 119, 122, 126-132, 134-141, 143-144, 146-150, 152, 154-159, 161-162, 164, 166-170, 172-182, 185, 188, 190-194, 196-200, 203, 206-207, 210-216, 220-221, 227, 232, 237-239, 243-244, 247, 249-252, 257-261

projected   153, 180, 188

projection   155

projects   2, 48, 105, 116, 126, 129, 134, 144, 147, 150, 155, 168-169, 181, 199, 201, 206, 215-217, 227, 243-244, 254

promising   113

promote   67, 169

promptly   128, 231

proofing   83

proper 95, 139, 254

properly   33, 127, 143, 152, 219, 254

proponents   236

proportion   260

proposal   162, 208

proposals   90, 169, 209

proposed   46, 53, 136, 143, 247-248, 251

protect 60, 109
protected 63
protection 104
protocols 182
provide 24, 68, 106, 123-124, 131, 142, 153, 163, 170, 173, 178, 182, 237, 239-240
provided 11, 96, 139, 175, 208, 225, 253
providers 75
provides 142, 166, 206
providing 95, 131, 162, 172, 180
provision 138, 193
provokes 212
public 135, 224
publisher 1
pulled 116
purchase 7, 208, 253
purchases 253
purchasing 253
purpose 2, 9, 116, 166, 172, 178, 223, 232, 239
pushing 113
qualified 36, 61-62, 64, 66, 69, 137, 146, 246
qualifies 63, 67
qualify 54, 59, 69
qualities 17, 234
quality 1, 4-5, 9, 23, 44, 56, 59, 64, 69-70, 81, 92, 95, 127, 138-139, 147, 155, 173, 177, 182, 184-186, 190, 206, 210, 215, 222, 224-226
quantified 98
quantify 54
quantities 208
question 10, 15, 27, 43, 58, 74, 89, 101, 108, 132, 135, 186, 235
questions 7-8, 10, 60, 170, 195, 235
quickly 9, 59, 67
radically 65
raters 234
rather 50, 115, 245
rating 209
rational 153
rationale 211, 223
reached 19
reactivate 102
readiness 34, 139
readings 94

realised   254
realistic   19, 68, 101, 136, 172
Reality 225, 231
realize 51
realized   102, 249
really   7, 24, 34, 141
reason 111, 198
reasonable   83, 111, 136, 155, 174, 254
reasonably   152, 209
reasons   38, 139, 154, 175, 185
reassess   138, 193
re-assign   160
reassigned   181
rebuild 113
receive   8-9, 30, 52
received   38, 117, 193, 210, 224
receivers   213
receives   234
receptive   254
recipient   19, 256
recognize   2, 15-17, 19-20, 23-24, 50, 77, 82, 168
recognized   16-17, 19, 21-23, 65, 195, 211, 240
recommend   111, 116, 147
recording   1, 229
records   62, 103, 153, 182-183, 224, 241, 253, 257
recovery   48
redefine   19, 32
re-design   66
reduce51, 54, 188, 198, 223, 231, 254
reducing   96, 111
referenced   184
references   262
reflect 69, 91, 93-94
reflected   240
reform 56, 90, 104, 118
reforms52-53
refuses 204
regarding   102, 120, 208, 216
Register   2, 4, 131, 141, 198, 203, 246
regret 80
regular 37-38, 65, 248
regularly   38, 215
regulatory   18, 245, 260

resource   3-4, 105, 134, 141, 152, 155, 160, 165-166, 169,
192, 210, 215-216, 229
resources   2, 7, 21-22, 25, 33, 36, 43, 64, 86, 92, 98-99, 103,
105, 112, 127-128, 133, 136, 152, 155, 157, 159-160, 163, 166, 170,
175, 179, 181, 210, 227, 237, 240, 242
respect   1
respond   188, 199, 230
responded   11
responding   198
response   21, 24, 91, 96-98, 248
responses   82, 104, 199
responsive   178
result   72, 84-85, 176, 179-180, 185, 221, 232, 256, 258
resulted   100
resulting   65, 135, 192
results   8, 34, 37, 50, 64, 74-77, 79, 81, 88, 96-97, 135, 139, 159,
178, 182, 187-188, 214-215, 233, 237, 249
Retain 101
retained   72
retrospect   116
return   84, 103, 163, 182
reused 203
revenue   22, 46
revenues   48
review 9, 34, 68, 163, 223, 225
reviewed   27, 149, 174
Reviewer   233
reviews139, 148, 188, 211
revised 72, 100, 152-153
revisions   256
revisit   223
Reward   51, 217
rewarded   22
rewards   94
rework 43, 183
rights   1
rolling   155
routine 93
routinely   188
safely   205
safety   112, 136
samples   182
sampling   182

CPSIA information can be obtained
at www.ICGtesting.com
Printed in the USA
BVHW082020110819
555624BV00016BA/1800/P